simple knits for cherished babies

erika knight

simple knits for cherished babies

photography by john heseltine

COLLINS & BROWN

First published in Great Britain in 2001 by Collins & Brown Limited,
London House, Great Eastern Wharf, Parkgate Road, London, SW11 4NQ

Distributed in the United States and Canada by Sterling Publishing Co,
387 Park Avenue South, New York, NY 10016

British Library Cataloguing-in-Publication Data:
A catalogue record for this title is available from the British Library.

9 8 7 6 5 4 3 2 1
ISBN 1 85585 926 2

A BERRY BOOK

Designer Debbie Mole
Editor Claire Waite Brown

Reproduction by Classic Scan Pte Ltd, Singapore
Printed and bound by Craft Print International Ltd, Singapore

This book was typeset using Frutiger and Bembo

contents:

A baby is a precious gift....

To cherish, nurture, celebrate, and care for,

To treasure, to protect,

To tend to, to hold dear, and to value.

Knitting for a new baby is always a great pleasure • The baby has a wonderful quality of newness, freshness and purity, and the whole joy and excitement of a new life creates a great rush of enthusiasm and creativity, as well as a desire to personalize the event • This desire to cherish, protect and nurture any young creature is very strong • How nice, then, if you can find some tangible way in which to express these feelings • Time is precious, so if someone knits for you, or you for them, the gift is very special • If a friend or relative is expecting a baby, it is a real pleasure to create something yourself, as an act of love, and then present it as a special gift for the new arrival – the smallness of the garments brings out the maternal instinct in all of us • Classically designed baby garments look as good in twenty years' time, creating heirloom pieces for a future generation of children.

This book contains a selection of traditional baby garments, with a slightly modern twist • The colour palette is soft, muted tones of chalky pastels, representing a return to more traditional colour values, and a move away from the primary colour brights of the last few years • There are three weights of yarn used: chunky, for hardwearing cardigans and blankets; medium for updated classic garments, and fine for garments chosen for their softness next to the skin: a tiny vest, for example, or a little pair of silk slippers for a new-born baby's delicate feet.

The design ideas in this book are informed by a few basic, but simple, rules • With tops for babies, any openings must go easily over the baby's head and the garments must slip on and off as easily as possible • The pattern instructions are written in simple language, without confusing abbreviations • The patterns generally contain few special techniques, and where these are required, a cross reference is made to an explanation at the back of the book • The only other referrals in the patterns are to charts, which are given for the relevant projects in a special section at the back of the book.

The stitches used in the projects contained in this book are simple: primarily stocking (stockinette) stitch, garter stitch and simple knit and purl rib, with a few special touches included to give these essentially plain garments a singularly beautiful finish. Casting on on a size smaller needle to produce a firmer edge, a few simple increasing and decreasing ideas to create a fully fashioned sleeve setting, a little picot trim or an integral button band, for example, can make a surprising difference to the finished look of the garment.

The yarns chosen for these patterns are all natural ones – cottons, silks and fine wools. They are soft and gentle on young skins, and they have the virtue of washing and wearing extremely well. Small enough to fit into a bag, the projects lend themselves to being knitted at odd moments – on planes, trains and buses, or in the lunch hour at work, or even while waiting in the wings at the hospital. It is important, particularly when knitting with delicate yarns in pale colours, to keep the work clean. While you knit, keep your needles, yarn and a copy of the pattern together in a simple bag (like the little organza one shown opposite) to protect your work It will do duty later as a gift bag.

Knitted gifts should be presented beautifully, as befits the trouble you have taken in making them, so take the time to pack up the garments or other projects attractively. Ideas are given on pages 106-7.

e r i k a **k** n i g h t

getting started

about **yarns and needles**

EACH BABY is special and unique, and the garments we make for them should echo these qualities and offer softness, warmth and protection. Time spent selecting delicate soft natural yarns suitable for babies will never be wasted, nor will the money spent on the best quality ones. Cashmere, silk, fine merino wool, and cotton, are a little more expensive to purchase than more traditionally available yarns designed for baby, but each have a very special quality. They provide luxurious softness to cocoon and cosset, and to keep baby warm in winter and cool in summer. Natural fibres allow the body to breathe, absorb moisture and circulate the air around baby's delicate body, and they wash and wear with a quality second to none. **Cashmere** is a noble fibre and the ultimate in luxury. It is ultra soft, light and beautiful to the touch. **Silk** has a renowned natural sheen and also an exquisite drape. It is luxurious and sensuous to the touch. **Fine merino wool** is strong and flexible, making it a joy to knit with as it creates a smooth, elegant fabric that keeps its shape well. It is warm in winter, cool in summer and does not crease. **Botany wool** is strong and light, but also warm. **Cotton** has a natural look and is soft and cool to the touch. It is available matt or shiny, smooth, slubby or textured. It is hardwearing and easy to wash. You need very little yarn to create garments for small babies. The tiny projects for new babies take just a ball or two of wool or silk. Depending on the size or weight of the yarn, you will need the appropriate needles. Bamboo needles are particularly suited to fine work, being wonderfully smooth. You will need relatively few sizes for the patterns in this book, the sizes needed being given at the start of each pattern.

about tension (gauge)

opposite: Graded from left to right, three principal weights of yarn – fine, medium and chunky – in cotton, silk and wool are shown with suitably sized bamboo needles along-side. The pattern instructions in the book explain which yarn weights and needle sizes are needed for each project.

IF YOU WANT THE PROJECTS you knit to be the correct size, your knitting must be the correct tightness or tension. Tension is the term given to the number of stitches and rows you should have to the centimetre/inch you knit on the given needles, yarn and stitch pattern. For accurate sizing, the tension must be correct. If you knit too tightly, your garment will be too small; if you knit too loosely, your garment will be too large. Every project instruction will give you the yarn, needles and tension required for that particular project. To check your tension, knit a sample square slightly larger than 10cm (4in) using the yarn, needles and stitch requested. Smooth the square out on a flat surface without stretching it. Then, using a ruler, mark out a 10cm (4in) square in the knitting and count every stitch and half stitch; check this number against the tension requested. Count the rows in the same way. If you have too many stitches and rows your knitting is too tight, and you will need to use a size fatter needle. If you have too few stitches and rows it is too loose, and you will need to knit with a size finer needle.

above: The same yarn is knitted on three different sizes of needle to illustrate how tension will affect the finished size of your project. The tension in the centre is the correct size. On the left the tension is too tight and on the right it is too loose. To adjust the tension, a change in needle size is needed.

about the patterns

THE PATTERNS IN THIS BOOK are written following normal pattern writing conventions. The instructions are written out in full, whenever possible, with as much information as it is feasible to give to make them easy to follow. Where there is a repeating instruction within the pattern, this passage is marked with asterisks. Where special techniques, such as increasing and decreasing or making an eyelet, are needed, this is indicated at the begining of the pattern and a cross-reference given to the explanation, which is listed at the back of the book on page 125. The technique is then incorporated into the pattern following the normal pattern writing convention.

sizing

Even new born babies vary greatly in size, from a premature baby weighing just a few pounds to an extra large baby whose birth weight is equal to that of a naturally small, three-month-old baby. It is important, therefore, not to go merely by age, but to work out actual sizes. If you are knitting in advance for a baby, guess at one of the middle sizes or, if the parents' family history indicates large babies, go for the biggest size – the baby will grow into it! Instructions are given in three sizes for each project, worked out on averages of age and weight but are intended as a guide only. In each pattern, the first instructions are given for the smallest size and the figures inside the brackets refer to the next sizes up. The sizing has been worked out to allow a little extra room for comfort. The three little vests shown here show the different sizes included in the instructions, 0 – 3 months, 3 – 6 months, 6 – 9 months. At the back of the book on pages 112-5 are details of the projects, with the actual baby measurements for which each size is intended, as well as the finished sizes of the knitted garments. To ensure the garments are the correct size, you should measure the baby first, if you can.

about trims & embellishments

JUST AS MUCH ATTENTION should be paid to the choice of trimmings as to the selection of yarn, as only too often a beautifully crafted garment is spoiled by inferior or cheap buttons or synthetic ribbon trims. It does take time to source interesting and beautiful trims and embellishments, but if you find it difficult to do through conventional stores you may chose to recycle from favourite discarded clothes or you can scour charity shops for the more unique and unusual items to personalize your projects. Most of the projects shown in this book are enhanced by the addition of the right trim in matching colours and suitable fabrics. Some of the simplest are the most delightful: organza ribbons in pale colours, washed–cotton tapes, fine decorative braids, tiny mother of pearl buttons, satin roses, cross–stitch embroidery, fine silk ribbons and antique lace. Take care when applying any trims or embellishments to do so as neatly as possible using appropriate matching thread and small, neat stitches.

warning

None of the garments or their trims must be dangerous for the baby in any way. Buttons must be securely fixed with button thread so that they cannot be pulled off and swallowed. Ribbons must be fixed in such a way that babies cannot choke on them or strangle themselves with them.

knitting for the baby

classic cashmere sweater

Cashmere is the ultimate yarn for comfort and luxury –

nothing but the best for the new addition to the family!

However, this simple stocking (stockinette) stitch sweater

can also be knitted in merino wool or cotton, if you prefer.

It is made in one piece, and is very easy to knit. The garter

stitch hems add a modern finishing touch, as do the

washed-cotton tape ties at the neck opening. The slit in

the centre back makes it really easy to slide the sweater

over the baby's head. The sweater can be combined with

the leggings (see page 26) and the bootees (see page 32)

to create a matching outfit for your baby.

how to make: classic cashmere sweater

SIZING: For sizing refer to chart on page 112.

MATERIALS: 3 (3:4) x 25g balls 4 ply yarn eg. Jaeger cashmere (which knits as a medium yarn) • Pair of 3³/₄mm (US 5) needles • Sewing needle • Cotton tape approximately 46cm (18in) in length • Sewing cotton to match tape

TENSION (GAUGE): 22 stitches and 32 rows to 10cm (4in) square measured over stocking (stockinette) stitch using 3³/₄mm (US 5) needles.

TECHNIQUES: Slip the first stitch

above: This is simple and easy to knit, worked in one piece. The slit at the back is made by dividing the stitches and working on each set of stitches in turn.

opposite: The soft natural luxury of cashmere, delicate "fashioned" detailing at the neck edge, the little garter stitch welt and the turned back cuffs (for growing room) are all classic features.

and knit the last stitch of every row on the sleeves; this will give a neat appearance when the sleeves are turned back. Cast on and cast off evenly, not too tightly, as this will ensure a neat edge. The only other technique required is knitting through the back of the loops (see page 125).

METHOD: Using 3³/₄mm (US 5) needles, cast on 52 (60:68) stitches. Work 6 rows in garter stitch; every row knit. Now change to stocking (stockinette) stitch and continue until work measures 12.5 (15:18)cm, 5 (6:7)in.

right: The neck opening is made by casting off the centre stitches and working on each set of stitches in turn. The shaping is worked two stitches in from the edge to give a soft, neat appearance.

below: To give a neat finish to the centre slit, the first stitch of every row is slipped onto the right needle.

opposite: When the garment is sewn up, the side seams are left unstitched at the garter stitch band to give a little side vent detail.

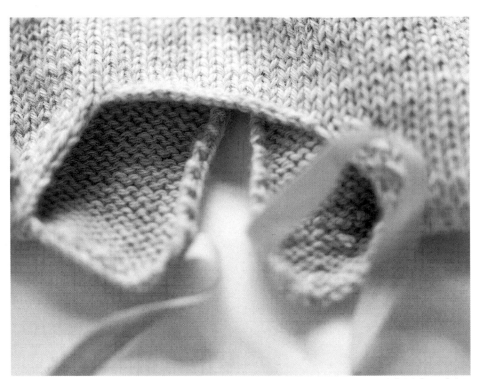

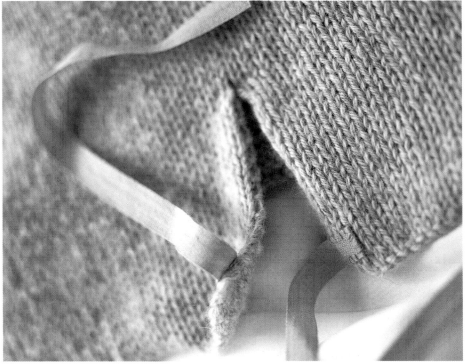

SHAPE SLEEVES: Cast on 34 (40:46) stitches at the beginning of the next 2 rows. *120 (140:160) stitches.* Continue on these stitches until the knitting measures 18.5 (22:25.5)cm, 7 (8^1/$_2$:10)in, ending with a purl row.

SHAPE NECK: Knit 53 (63:72) stitches, cast off the centre 14 (14:16) stitches, knit to the end of the row. Now work on each set of stitches in turn.
Row 1: slip the first stitch, purl to end (neck edge).
Row 2: knit 2 stitches, knit the next 2 stitches together through the back loops, knit to the end of the row. Work these last 2 rows twice more. Work straight until knitting measures 21.5 (25:29)cm, 8^1/$_2$ (10:11^1/$_2$)in, ending with a purl row.

TO MAKE THE CENTRE BACK SPLIT: Cast on 11 (11:12) stitches at the beginning of the next row. Now work on these 61 (71:81) stitches for a further 7 (8:9)cm, 2³/₄ (3¹/₄: 3³/₄)in, ending with a purl row. Break yarn and leave the stitches on the needle or a length of yarn.

NOW WORK THE OTHER SIDE: With the wrong side of the work facing, rejoin yarn to neck edge and purl to the last stitch, knit it. **Row 1:** knit to the last 4 stitches, knit 2 stitches together, knit 2 stitches. **Row 2:** purl to the last stitch, knit it. Work these last 2 rows twice more. Work straight until the knitting measures 21.5 (25:29)cm, 8¹/₂ (10:11¹/₂)in, ending with a knit row. Cast on 11 (11:12) stitches at the beginning of the next row. Now work on these 61 (71:81) stitches for a further 7 (8:9)cm, 2³/₄ (3¹/₄:3³/₄)in, ending with a purl row. **Next**

row: knit across all the stitches from both halves, knitting the 2 centre stitches together. *121 (141:161) stitches.* Work straight until knitting measures 9 (10:11.5)cm, 3¹/₂ (4: 4¹/₂)in from back neck edge. Cast off 34 (40:46) stitches at the beginning of the next 2 rows. *53 (61:69) stitches.* Continue to knit for a further 10.5 (13:16)cm, 4¹/₄ (5:6¹/₄)in. Work 6 rows in garter stitch, every row knit. Cast off.

TO FINISH: Sew in all ends by weaving along the knitting, not up the side. Lay work out flat and steam gently. Sew side and sleeve seams, leaving the garter stitch band unsewn to form a little vent detail. Cut the length of cotton tape in half, fold under 1cm (¹/₂in) of one end of the tape and oversew onto one side of the back neck split. Repeat for other side. Tie tapes into a bow.

classic cashmere leggings

Although you see them less frequently nowadays, leggings are extremely useful in cold weather. They bring back memories of post-war babies and sepia-tinted photographs. These particular leggings are reworked in soft, luxurious cashmere, making them uniquely comfortable for your baby, although they could be equally easily knitted in merino wool or cotton. The leggings can be adjusted to fit at the waist with washed-cotton tapes threaded through eyelet holes. The feet to the leggings have attractive fully fashioned detailing. Combine them with the cashmere sweater (see page 20) and the bootees (see page 32), if you knit them without the feet, for a complete outfit.

how to make: classic cashmere leggings

opposite: These classic leggings are worked in softest cashmere, with delicate fashioned detailing, garter stitch feet and washed-cotton tape ties.

SIZING: For sizing refer to chart on page 112.

MATERIALS: 3 (3:4) x 25g balls 4 ply yarn, e.g. Jaeger cashmere (knits as medium) • Pair of 3³/₄mm (US 5) needles • Pair of 3¹/₄mm (US 3) needles • Sewing needle • Cotton tape approximately 84 cm (33in) long

TENSION (GAUGE): 22 stitches and 32 rows to 10 cm (4in) measured over stocking (stockinette) stitch using 3³/₄mm (US 5) needles.

TECHNIQUES: A few simple techniques are needed for these leggings. Increasing and decreasing, worked two stitches in from the edge, to give a fully fashioned look; knitting through the back of the loops, making an eyelet by taking the yarn over and picking up stitches. These are all explained in more detail on page l25.

METHOD: RIGHT LEG: start at waistline. Using 3¹/₄mm (US 3) needles, cast on 58 (62:66) stitches and work 3 rows in rib as follows: Every row: knit 1 stitch, purl 1 stitch alternately to the end of the row.

MAKE EYELETS: Next row: knit 1 stitch, purl 1 stitch, ★ yarn over, purl 2 stitches together, knit 1 stitch, purl 1 stitch: repeat from ★ to the end of the row. Work 3 more rows in rib as set.
Change to 3³/₄mm (US 5) needles and stocking (stockinette) stitch. Then work as follows: **Row 1:** knit **Row 2:** purl.

WORK BACK SHAPING ROWS: Row 1: knit 10 (12:14) stitches, turn, purl 10 (12:14) stitches. **Row 2:** knit 16 (18:20) stitches, turn, purl 16 (18:20) stitches. **Row 3:** knit 22 (24:26) stitches, turn, purl 22 (24:26) stitches. Continue like this, working 6 extra stitches on every row until the row knit 40 (42:44) stitches, turn, purl 40 (42:44) stitches has been worked. ★★ Continue to work in stocking (stockinette) stitch, across all the stitches. Increase at each end of the 5 (5:7)th row and then every following 10th row until there are 68 (72:76) stitches. Work straight, without any further shaping, until the front seam (the short edge of the work) measures 18 (20: 23)cm, 7 (8:9)in, ending with a purl row. Place coloured threads at each end of the last row.

SHAPE LEG: Row 1: knit 1 stitch, knit 2 stitches together through the back loops, knit to the last 3 stitches, knit 2 stitches together, knit 1 stitch. **Row 2:** purl 1 stitch, purl 2 stitches together, purl to last 3 stitches, purl 2 stitches together through the back loops, purl 1 stitch. Repeat these 2 rows twice more. *56 (60:64) stitches.*
Now decrease 1 stitch at each end of the next and every following third row until 28 (32:36) stitches remain. Work straight until leg measures 16 (18:20)cm, 6 (7:8) in from the coloured markers, ending with a purl row. ★★

DIVIDE FOR THE FOOT: Knit 23 (26:29) stitches, turn. Purl 9 (9:11) stitches, turn. Work 14 (18:22) rows stocking (stockinette) stitch on these 9 (9:11) stitches. Break yarn. With right side facing, rejoin the yarn to the

left: Simple eyelets holes are worked by making an extra stitch and then knitting the next two stitches together. Cotton tape is then threaded through the holes and tied loosely at the front.

inside edge of 14 (17:18) stitches and pick up and knit 7 (9:11) stitches along the side of the foot, knit across the 9 (9:11) stitches on the needle, pick up and knit 7 (9:11) stitches along the other side of the foot, knit across remaining 5 (6:7) stitches. *42 (50:58) stitches*. Knit 7 (9:9) rows.

SHAPE FOOT: **Row 1:** knit 14 (18:22) stitches, knit 2 stitches together, knit 1 stitch, knit 2 stitches together, knit 16 (20:24) stitches, knit 2 stitches together, knit 1 stitch, knit 2 stitches together, knit 2 stitches. **Row 2:** knit. **Row 3:** knit 13 (17:21) stitches, knit 2 stitches together, knit 1 stitch, knit 2 stitches together, knit 14 (18:22) stitches, knit 2 stitches together, knit 1 stitch, knit 2 stitches together, knit 1 stitch. **Row 4:** knit. **Row 5:** knit 12 (16:20) stitches, knit 2 stitches together, knit 1 stitch, knit 2 stitches together, knit 12 (16:20) stitches, knit 2 stitches together, knit 1 stitch, knit 2 stitches together. Cast off.

LEFT LEG: Using 3¼mm (US 3) needles, cast on 58 (62:66) stitches and work rib and eyelets as for right leg. Change to 3¾mm (US 5) needles and work in stocking (stockinette) stitch as follows: **Next row:** knit.
WORK BACK SHAPING ROWS: **Row 1:** purl 10 (12:14) stitches, turn, knit 10 (12:14) stitches. **Row 2:** purl 16 (18:20) stitches, turn, knit 16 (18:20) stitches. **Row 3:** purl 22 (24:26) stitches, turn, knit 22 (24:26) stitches. Continue like this, working 6 extra stitches on every row until the row purl 40 (42:44) stitches, turn, knit 40 (42:44) stitches has been worked. **Next row:** purl to the end. Now work from ★★ to ★★ as on right leg.

left: The leg seam and foot seam are joined in one straight continuous line. The garter stitch gives shape to the sole.

DIVIDE FOR THE FOOT: knit 14 (17:18) stitches, turn. Purl 9 (9:11) stitches, turn. Work 14 (18:22) rows in stocking (stockinette) stitch on these 9 (9:11) stitches. Break yarn. With right side facing, rejoin the yarn to the inside edge of 5 (6:7) stitches and pick up and knit 7 (9:11) stitches along the side of the foot, knit across 9 (9:11) stitches on the needle, pick up and knit 7 (9:11) stitches along the other side of the foot, knit across the remaining 14 (17:18) stitches. *42 (50:58) stitches.* Knit 7 (9:9) rows.

SHAPE THE FOOT: Row 1: knit 2 stitches, knit 2 stitches together, knit 1 stitch, knit 2 stitches together, knit 16 (20:24) stitches, knit 2 stitches together, knit 1 stitch, knit 2 stitches together, knit 14 (18:22) stitches. **Row 2:** knit. **Row 3:** knit 1 stitch, knit 2 stitches together, knit 1 stitch, knit 2 stitches together, knit 14 (18:22) stitches, knit 2 stitches together, knit 1 stitch, knit 2 stitches together, knit 13 (17:21) stitches. **Row 4:** knit. **Row 5:** knit 2 stitches together, knit 1 stitch, knit 2 stitches together, knit 12 (16:20) stitches, knit 2 stitches together, knit 1 stitch, knit 2 stitches together, knit 12 (16:20) stitches. Cast off.

TO FINISH: Sew in all ends by weaving them along the knitting, not up the side. Lay work out flat and steam gently. With right sides together pin and sew the back and front seams to the markers, then sew up the inside leg and finally the foot seams, noting the seam is on the side of the foot. Thread tape through the eyelet holes, and tie in a bow.

classic cashmere bootees

These little bootees are ideal for both very young babies and those just beginning to get to their feet. Knitted in cashmere, they are soft and gentle on the delicate skin of the baby's feet, although they can equally well be knitted in merino wool or cotton. The simple roll edge gives the classic pattern a modern touch. The techniques required for these bootees are not difficult – you simply need to be able to pick up a few stitches. They make the perfect gift for a baby shower, and can be added to the sweater (see page 20) and the leggings (see page 26) if you knit the latter without the feet.

how to make: classic cashmere bootees

SIZING: For sizing refer to chart on page 112.

MATERIALS: 1 (1:1) x 25g ball 4 ply yarn, e.g. Jaeger cashmere (knits as medium) or Rowan wool/cotton • Pair of 3³/₄mm (US 5) needles • Safety pin

TENSION (GAUGE): 24 stitches and 32 rows to 10cm (4in) square measured over stocking (stockinette) stitch using 3³/₄mm (US 5) needles.

TECHNIQUES: For this project you need to be able to pick up stitches. An explanation of how to do so is given on page l25.

top left: Working on the centre set of stitches to make the top of the foot. A spare needle or large safety pins may be useful for holding the stitches not in use.

top right: Stitches along the sides and the edge are picked up and worked in garter stitch to make the sole.

METHOD: With 3³/₄mm (US 5) needles cast on 29 (33:37) stitches and work 10 (10:12) rows stocking (stockinette) stitch. **Next row:** knit 19 (22: 25) stitches, turn. **Next row:** purl 9 (11:13) stitches, turn. On 9 (11:13) stitches, work 14 (14:16) rows in stocking (stockinette) stitch. Break yarn. With right side of work facing, rejoin yarn to the inside edge of the 10 (11:12) stitches and pick up and knit 7 (9:11) stitches along the side of the foot, knit across 9 (11:13) stitches on the needle, pick up and knit 7 (9:11) stitches along the other side of the foot, and finally knit across the remaining 10 (11:12) stitches. *43 (51:59) stitches.* Work 7 (9:11) rows of garter stitch, every row knit.

SHAPE THE FOOT: **Row 1:** knit 2 stitches, knit 2 stitches together, knit 15 (19:23) stitches, knit 2 stitches together, knit 1 stitch, knit 2 stitches together, knit 15 (19:23) stitches, knit 2 stitches together, knit 2 stitches. **Row 2:** knit. **Row 3:** knit 2 stitches, knit 2 stitches together, knit 13 (17:21) stitches, knit 2 stitches together, knit 1 stitch, knit 2 stitches together, knit 13 (17:21) stitches, knit 2 stitches together, knit 2 stitches. **Row 4:** knit. **Row 5:** knit 2 stitches, knit 2 stitches together. Knit 11 (15:19) stitches, knit 2 stitches together, knit 1 stitch, knit 2 stitches together, knit 11 (15:19) stitches knit 2 stitches together, knit 2 stitches. Cast off.

TO MAKE UP: Weave in all ends along the work, not up the side as this will cause a lumpy edge. Lay work out and gently steam. Join the heel and the foot with a flat seam. Roll over the top edge and stitch down at the back seam with a single stitch to keep the roll edge in position.

below: A simple first gift for the new baby, these little bootees can be made in a night or even on the way to work. The simple roll edge gives a modern touch to a traditional bootee pattern. Knit them in cashmere or the finest merino wool for the ultimate in comfort for baby's tiny toes. Alternatively, make them in cotton for a summer arrival.

garter stitch cardigan

This is one of the simplest patterns of all, knitted in garter stitch in double knit yarn throughout, in one piece, with simple garter stitch bands at the front and the sleeve hems. The only technique involved is creating the simple buttonholes in the front bands. Five small, neat buttons fasten the cardigan, and the V-neck makes it very comfortable for the baby to wear. Knit it in cotton or wool, or a mixture of both, for all-year-round comfort.

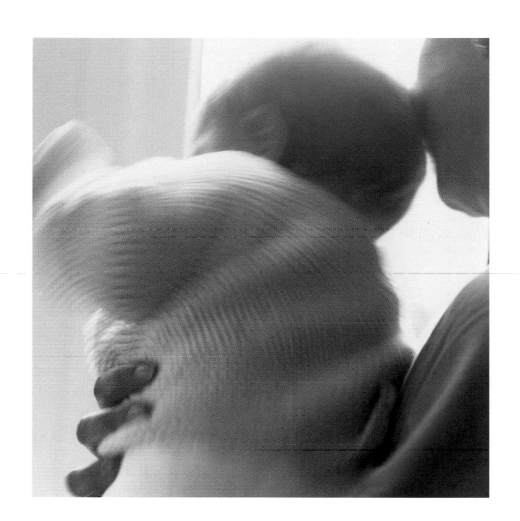

how to make: garter stitch cardigan

SIZE: For sizing refer to chart on page 113.

MATERIALS: 3 x 50g balls double knit yarn, e.g. Rowan wool/cotton or Rowan double knit cotton • Pair of $3^3/_4$mm (US 5) needles • Pair of 4mm (US 6) needles • 5 buttons • Stitch holder • Sewing needle

TENSION (GAUGE): 22 stitches and 36 rows to 10cm (4in) square measured over garter stitch using 4mm (US 6) needles.

TECHNIQUES: The special techniques are increasing and decreasing, and picking up stitches (see page 125).

METHOD: Using $3^3/_4$mm (US 5) needles, cast on 50 (56:62) stitches. Work 5 rows in garter stitch, every row knit. Change to 4mm (US 6) needles and continue until work measures 12 (13.5:15)cm, $4^3/_4$ ($5^1/_2$:6)in.

SHAPE SLEEVES: Cast on 17 (19:21) stitches at the beginning of the next 2 rows. *84 (94:104) stitches.*

Continue until work measures 21 (23:25)cm, $8^1/_4$ (9:$9^3/_4$)in.

WORK RIGHT FRONT AND SLEEVE: Knit 30 (34:38) stitches, turn and leave remaining 54 (60:66) stitches on a stitch holder.
★ Working on 30 (34:38) stitches, knit 4 (4:6) rows straight, increase at neck edge on next and every alternate row until there are 41 (46:51) stitches on needle. Continue straight until sleeve measures 18 (19:20)cm, 7 ($7^1/_2$:8)in in depth, ending at sleeve edge. Cast off 17 (19:21) stitches and continue on the remaining 24 (27:30) stitches until work measures 41 (45:49)cm, 16 ($17^3/_4$:$19^1/_4$)in. Change to $3^3/_4$mm (US 5) needles, knit 5 rows. Cast off.

WORK LEFT FRONT AND SLEEVE: Place 24 (26:28) stitches on stitch holder for back neck. Rejoin the yarn to the remaining 30 (34:38) stitches at neck edge, and knit to the end of the row. Work from ★ to match the first side.

above left: Knitted in medium-weight yarn, such as merino wool or cotton, or a blend of both, this little cardigan is very quick and easy to make.

above right: The stitches are picked up along the fronts and the neck edge to give a neat finish and small eyelet buttonholes are made in the garter stitch band.

right: Fastened with tiny mother of pearl buttons and updated with three-quarter length sleeves, this garter stitch cardigan is a timeless and versatile favourite.

right: garter stitch makes a wonderfully textural fabric, which is also the easiest of all to knit. Heavier weight yarns help to emphasize this textural quality.

SLEEVE BANDS: With right side of work facing, using $3^3/_4$mm (US 5) needles, pick up 37 (41:45) stitches along the sleeve edge. Knit 4 rows. Cast off.

FRONT BAND: Using $3^3/_4$mm (US 5) needles and with right side of work facing, pick up 31 (35:39) stitches up right front, 15 (16:19) stitches up right neck, 24 (26:28) stitches from stitch holder, 15 (16:18) stitches down left neck and 31 (35:39) stitches down left front. *116 (128:144) stitches.* Knit 2 rows.

TO MAKE BUTTONHOLES: Knit to last 33 (37:41) stitches ★ yarn forward, knit 2 stitches together, knit 5(6:7) stitches, repeat from ★ three more times, yarn forward, knit 2 stitches together, knit to the end. Knit 1 row, then cast off.

TO MAKE UP: Weave in all ends. Lay work out flat and gently steam. With the right sides of the knitting facing, sew up the sleeve and side seams using simple overstitch, leaving the sides open 2.5cm (1in) at the bottom to make a vent detail. Sew on the buttons to correspond with the buttonholes.

personalized baby blanket

This wonderfully soft baby blanket, knitted in a very soft cotton blend, relies on its exquisite texture and classic design for its appeal. Knitted in stocking (stockinette) stitch, with a raised garter stitch border, it can be knitted easily and quickly by the most inexperienced knitter. To add character to the blanket, a monogrammed B for baby can be positioned in the centre of the blanket by simply reversing the stitches from knit to purl to form the letter. If you prefer you could work the baby's initial instead. Charts for this purpose are given at the back of the book.

how to make: **personalized baby blanket**

SIZE: This blanket measures 90cm (36in) x 74cm (29in)

MATERIALS: 6 x 50g balls chunky yarn, eg Rowan all seasons cotton • Pair of 4¹/₂mm (US 7) needles • Sewing needle

TENSION (GAUGE): 18 stitches and 25 rows to 10cm (4in) square measured over stocking (stockinette) stitch using 4¹/₂mm (US 7) needles

TECHNIQUES: Always start a new ball of yarn at the beginning of a row, not in the middle. You need to follow the chart on page 116.

METHOD: With 4¹/₂mm (US 7) needles cast on 130 stitches and work 7 rows in garter stitch, every row knit. Change to stocking (stockinette) stitch with garter stitch edges as follows: **Row 1:** knit all stitches. **Row 2:** knit 5 stitches, purl to the last 5 stitches, knit 5 stitches. Repeat

above: A detail of the garter stitch border to the blanket, which helps to give it a solid, firm edge.

opposite: The initial B is created in the centre of the blanket by simply reversing stitches from knit to purl. It creates not only the letter itself, but an interesting texture to the surface. The heavier weight yarn knits up quickly, making this an easy yet effective project to make for the nursery or the stroller.

rows 1 and 2 forty seven times. *96 rows.*

With the right side of the work facing you, work the letter 'B' for baby by referring to the 24 stitches and 32 rows from the chart, on page 116. (Charts for other letters are given on the following pages).

Row 1: knit 53 stitches; working from the chart for 'B', knit 5 stitches, purl 19 stitches; knit to the end. **Row 2:** knit 5 stitches, purl 48 stitches; working from the chart for 'B', knit 20 stitches, purl 4 stitches; purl to the last 5 stitches, knit 5 stitches. This places the letter in the centre of the blanket. Continue to work from the chart, working odd number rows from right to left and even number rows from left to right. When you have worked the letter chart, work another 95 rows in stocking (stockinette) stitch with garter stitch edges, ending with the wrong side facing you. Work 7 rows in garter stitch. Cast off.

TO FINISH: Sew in any loose ends. Gently steam and press the knitting flat.

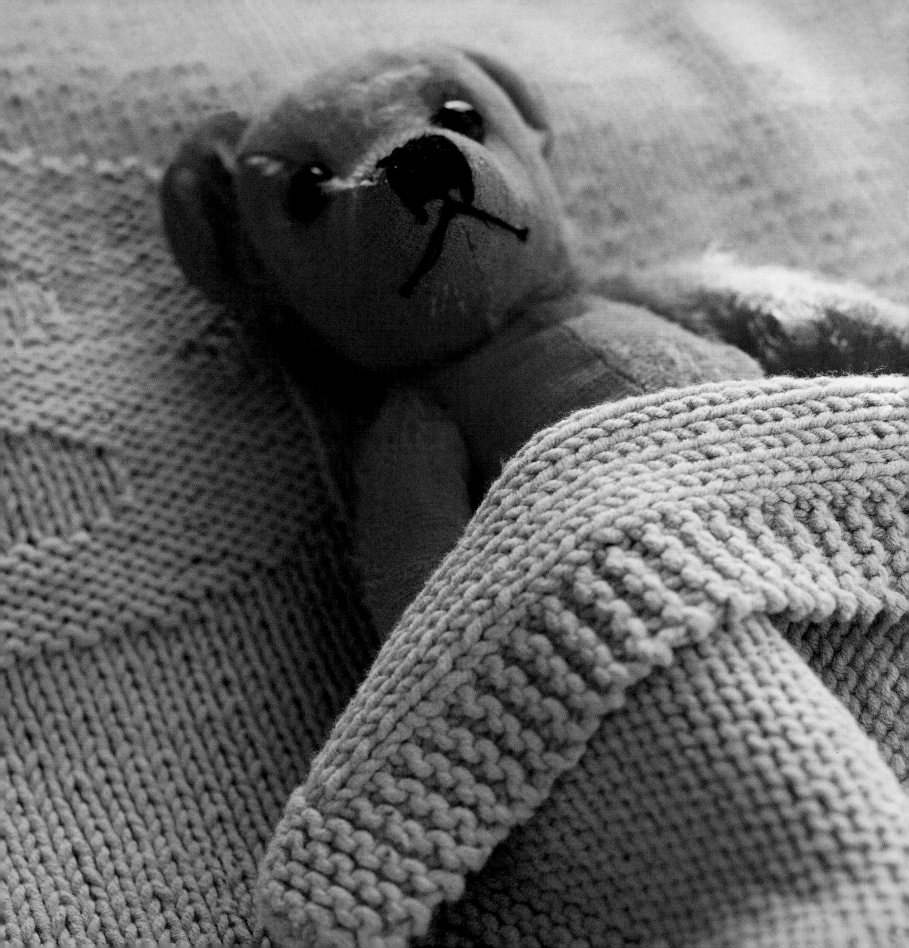

personalized baby cushion

This is very simple and quick to knit in a mixture of stocking (stockinette) stitch and garter stitch. Very similar to the baby blanket in design, the cushion features a prominent initial in the centre created reversed out of the stocking (stockinette) stitch. Charts for other initials are given at the back of the book. This cushion is knitted in a chunky cotton blend that is both light and soft. The simple garter stitch edging creates a smart finishing touch, as does the simple garter stitch panel on the back opening.

how to make: personalized baby cushion

SIZE: This cushion measures 40cm (16in) square.

MATERIALS: 5 x 50g balls chunky yarn, e.g. Rowan all seasons cotton • Pair of $4^1/2$mm (US 7) needles • Sewing needle • 40cm (16in) square cushion pad.

TENSION (GAUGE): 18 stitches x 25 rows to 10cm (4in) square measured over stocking (stockinette) stitch using $4^1/2$mm (US 7) needles.

TECHNIQUES: Always start a new ball of yarn at beginning of a row, not in the middle. You need to follow the chart for the intial shown on page 116.

METHOD: With $4^1/2$mm (US 7) needles cast on 72 stitches and work 7 rows in garter stitch, every row knit. Change to stocking (stockinette) stitch with garter stitch edges. **Row 1:** knit. **Row 2:** knit 5 stitches, purl to the last 5 stitches, knit 5 stitches. Repeat rows 1 and 2 until work measures 27cm ($10^3/4$in), ending with a knit row. Change to garter stitch and work 7 rows.
Change to stocking (stockinette) stitch with garter stitch edges as before and work 26 rows. With the right side of the knitting facing you, work the letter B for baby by referring to the 24 stitches and 32 rows

top left: Stitch the two layers together at each side using the same yarn, matching the ridges of the garter stitch to ensure a neat finish.

top right: The simple garter stitch band creates a firm and decorative edge for the centre back opening of the cushion and requires no fastening.

opposite: This little cushion makes a nice personal touch for the baby either in the nursery or for the stroller.

from the chart on page 116. **Row 1:** knit 24 stitches; working from the chart for 'B', knit 5 stitches, purl 19 stitches, then knit to end. **Row 2:** knit 5 stitches, purl 19 stitches; working from the chart for 'B', knit 20 stitches, purl 4 stitches; purl to last 5 stitches, knit 5 stitches. This places the letter in the centre of the cushion. Continue to work from the chart, working odd number rows from right to left and even number rows from left to right. When you have worked the letter chart, next work another 27 rows in stocking (stockinette) stitch with garter stitch edges, ending with the wrong side of the knitting facing you. Work 7 rows in garter stitch. Change to stocking (stockinette) stitch with garter stitch edges and work 40 rows. Work 7 rows in garter stitch. Cast off.

TO FINISH: Weave in all ends. Lay work out flat, steam and press gently. With the right side of the work facing, fold the work in towards the centre from the first horizontal garter stitch bands, stitch the two layers together at each side using the same yarn and mattress stitch (see page 125). Now fold knitting in from third horizontal garter stitch band and stitch the seams as before sewing through all the thickness of the overlapping pieces to make an 'envelope'. Turn right side out and place cushion pad inside.

chunky knit cardigan

This is another classic cardigan pattern for a baby, but given a modern twist thanks to the chunky, quick-to-knit cotton yarn used for it. Simple rib trims are used for the front button bands and for the sleeve hems, and the raglan sleeves have an unusual and attractive, fully fashioned decreasing detail. This simple cardigan can be knitted as an outfit with the beanie hat on page 54.

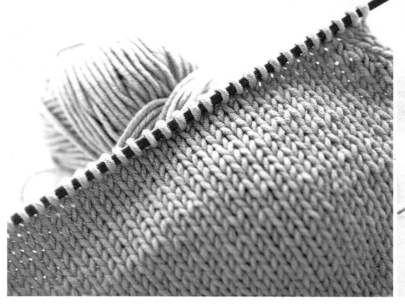

how to make: chunky knit cardigan

SIZING: For sizing refer to chart on page 113.

MATERIALS: 3 (3:4) x 50g balls chunky yarn, e.g. Rowan all seasons cotton • Pair of 4mm (US 6) needles • Pair of 4¹/₂mm (US 7) needles • Sewing needle • 3 buttons • Safety pin.

TENSION (GAUGE): 18 stitches and 25 rows to 10cm (4in) square measured over stocking (stockinette) stitch using 4¹/₂mm (US 7) needles.

TECHNIQUES: The only special techniques involved are increasing and decreasing and knitting through the back of the loops (see page 125).

METHOD: Using 4 mm (US 6) needles cast on 40 (44: 50) stitches and work 2cm (1in) in simple rib stitch as follows: **Every row:** ★ knit 1 stitch, purl 1 stitch, repeat from ★ to end. Change to 4¹/₂mm (US 7) needles and work in stocking (stockinette) stitch until knitting measures 9 (11:13)cm, 3¹/₂ (4¹/₄:5)in from the cast on edge.

top left: Heavier weight cotton yarn makes this a quick design to knit up and the roundness of the yarn gives clarity to the simple stitch.

top right: Knit the decrease stitches three stitches in from the edge. This will give a softer shape and a modern "fashioned" detail to this simple classic design.

opposite: This design can be worked in cotton or wool and be made for either girl or boy.

SHAPE ARMHOLES: Cast off 2 stitches at the beginning of the next 2 rows. **Next row:** knit 3 stitches, knit 2 stitches together, knit to the last 5 stitches, knit 2 stitches together through the back of the loops, knit to the end. Decrease 1 stitch at each end of the next 3 knit rows, in the same way. *28:(32:38) stitches.* Continue straight until work measures 17 (19:22)cm, 6³/₄ (7¹/₂:8³/₄) in.

SHAPE SHOULDERS: Cast off 7 (8:10) stitches at the beginning of the next 2 rows. Leave the remaining stitches on a safety pin to pick up later.

WORK LEFT FRONT: With 4mm (US 6) needles cast on 19 (21:24) stitches. Work 2cm (1in) in simple rib as on back. Change to 4¹/₂mm (US 7) needles and work in stocking (stockinette) stitch until knitting measures 9(11:13) cm, 3¹/₂ (4¹/₄: 5)in, ending with a purl row. ★★

SHAPE ARMHOLE: Cast off 2 stitches at the beginning the next row, knit to end. **Next row:** purl to the last 5 stitches, purl 2 stitches together, purl 3 stitches. Now decrease 1 stitch on each purl row 3 more times in this same way. *13 (15: 18) stitches.*

SHAPE NECK (RIGHT SIDE FACING): **Row 1:** knit to last 5 stitches, knit 2 stitches together, knit 3 stitches. **Row 2:** purl 3 stiches, purl 2 stitches together, purl to end. **Row 3:** as row 1. **Row 4:** purl. Repeat rows 3 and 4 until 7 (8:10) stitches remain. Continue without shaping until work measures l7 (l9:22)cm, $6^{3}/_{4}$ ($7^{1}/_{2}$: $8^{3}/_{4}$)in, ending with a purl row. Cast off.

WORK RIGHT FRONT: Work as the left front to ★★.

SHAPE ARMHOLE: **Row 1:** knit. **Row 2:** cast off 2 stitches, purl to end. **Row 3:** knit to last 5 stiches, knit 2 stitches together through the back of the loops, knit 3 stitches. **Row 4:** purl. **Rows 5–8:** repeat rows 3 and 4 twice more. *14 (16:19) stitches.* **Row 9:** knit 3 stitches, knit 2 stitches

together through the back loops, knit to last 5 stitches, knit 2 stitches together through the back loops, knit 3 stitches. **Row 10:** purl to the last 5 stitches, purl 2 stitches together through the back loops, purl 3 stitches. Continue decreasing on neck edge **only** as set on each **knit** row until 7 (8:10) stitches remain. Continue without shaping until work measures 17 (19:22)cm, $6^{3}/_{4}$ ($7^{1}/_{2}$:$8^{3}/_{4}$)in, ending with a purl row. Cast off.

SLEEVES: *make 2 the same.* With 4 mm (US 6) needles cast on 23 (25:27) stitches. Work 2cm (1in) in simple rib stitch as on back. Change to $4^{1}/_{2}$mm (US 7) needles and stocking (stockinette) stitch. Increase 1 stitch at each end of the first row and every 6th row that follows to 29 (31:33) stitches. Continue straight until the knitting measures 12.5 (15:18)cm, 5 (6:7)in.

SHAPE TOP: Cast off 2 stitches at the beginning of the next 2 rows. **Row 1:** knit 3 stitches, knit 2 stitches together, knit to the last 5 stitches, knit 2 stitches together through the back of the loops, knit 3 stitches. **Row 2:** purl. Repeat rows 1 and 2 until l7 (19:21) stitches remain. Cast off 3 stitches at the beginning of the next 4 rows. *(5:7:9) stitches.*

TO MAKE UP: Sew in all ends. Lay pieces out flat and steam and press gently. From the right side of the work join shoulder seams taking one stitch from the back and one from the front alternately.

FRONT BAND: With 4mm (US 6) needles and the right side of the knitting facing you, pick up and knit 20 (22:25) stitches up the right front, 13 (14:15) stitches up the V-slope, 16 (20: 22) stitches from safety pin, 13 (14:15) stitches down the V-slope, 20 (22:25) stitches down the left front. *82 (92:102) stitches.* Work 2 rows knit 1 stitch, purl 1 stitch rib. **Next row:** make 3 buttonholes as follows: Rib 2 stitches ★ yarn over, purl 2 stitches together, rib 6 (8:10) stitches. Repeat from ★ twice more, rib to the end. Work 1 more row in rib. Then cast off.

TO FINISH: Set the sleeves in between the armhole shapings. Stitch in place. Sew the sleeve and side seams. Sew on the 3 buttons to correspond with the buttonholes.

baby's beanie hat

This little pull-on hat is very quick and easy to knit. If you knit it in the same chunky cotton yarn as the cardigan on page 50 it makes an attractive outfit for the baby. The simple roll-edged brim allows you to adjust the size to fit the baby's head, and the stocking (stockinette) stitch and simple shaping are very easy to work. The hat is knitted on two needles, with a back seam.

how to make: baby's beanie hat

opposite: This is easily and quickly knitted in stocking (stockinette) stitch on two needles. Use a size smaller needle to cast on to give a neater roll edge. The shaping is created by knitting two stitches together at intervals on the knit rows.

SIZING: For sizing refer to chart on page 113.

MATERIALS: 1 (1:1) x 50g ball chunky yarn, e.g. Rowan all seasons cotton • Pair of 4mm (US 6) needles • Pair of 4¹/₂mm (US 7) needles • Sewing needle.

TENSION (GAUGE): 18 stitches and 25 rows to 10cm (4in) square measured over stocking (stockinette) stitch using 4¹/₂mm (US 7) needles.

TECHNIQUES: No special techniques required.

METHOD: With 4mm (US 6) needles, cast on 61 (68:75) stitches and work 4 rows in stocking (stockinette) stitch. Change to 4¹/₂mm (US 7) needles and work 16 (18:20) rows in stocking (stockinette) stitch. Now decrease as follows: **Decrease row 1:** ★ knit 8 stitches, knit 2 stitches together, repeat from ★ to last 1 (8:5) stitches, knit 1 (8:5) stitches. Work 3 rows in stocking (stockinette) stitch. **Decrease row 2:** ★ knit 7 stitches, knit 2 stitches together, repeat from ★ to last 1 (8:5) stitches, knit 1 (8:5) stitches. Work 3 rows in stocking (stockinette) stitch. **Decrease row 3:** ★ knit 6 stitches, knit 2 stitches together, repeat from ★ to last 1 (0:5) stitches, knit 1 (0:5) stitches. Work 3 rows in stocking (stockinette) stitch. **Decrease row 4:** ★ knit 5 stitches, knit 2 stitches together, repeat from ★ to last 1 (0:5) stitches, knit 1 (0:5) stitches. Purl 1 row. **Decrease row 5:** ★ knit 4 stitches, knit 2 stitches together, repeat from ★ to last 1 (0:5) stitches, knit 1 (0:5) stitches. Purl 1 row. **Decrease row 6:** ★ knit 3 stitches, knit 2 stitches together, repeat from ★ to last 1 (0:0) stitch, knit 1 (0:0) stitch. Purl 1 row. **Decrease row 7:** ★ knit 2 stitches, knit 2 stitches together, repeat from ★ to last 1 (0:0) stitch, knit 1 (0:0) stitch. Purl 1 row. **Decrease row 8:** knit 2 stitches together across row to last 1 (1:0) stitch, knit 1 (1:0). Leave length of yarn (for sewing) and break yarn. With the wrong side of the work facing you, thread yarn through the remaining stitches, pull up and sew to secure.

TO FINISH: Sew the seam. Gently steam and roll brim to required length, and catch down at back to secure the brim into position.

garter stitch wrap top

This exquisitely simple wrap top is ideal for a new baby. It is
knitted in silk, which is wonderfully soft for the baby to snuggle
into and exactly the right choice of yarn for a new baby's delicate
and sensitive skin. You can knit it in white, or in light silvery grey

or a muted soft pink. Match it with a pair of the silk slippers (see

page 80) for an heirloom gift for a new baby or as a present for a

special celebration. Organza ribbons, fastened at the back, keep

the top snugly in place.

how to make: garter stitch wrap top

SIZING: For sizing refer to chart on page 114.

MATERIALS: 1 (2:2) x 25g balls fine yarn, e.g. Jaeger 4 ply silk, Jaeger Siena 100% cotton or Rowan true 4 ply botany • Pair of 3mm (US 2) needles • Sewing needle • Organza ribbon, 1cm ($\frac{1}{2}$in) wide and 60cm (24in) long.

TENSION (GAUGE): 28 stitches and 48 rows to 10cm (4in) square measured over garter stitch using 3mm (US 2) needles.

TECHNIQUES: Slip the first stitch and knit the last stitch of every row to give a neat edge. Work the cast on edge with a size smaller needle to give a neat firm edge. The only other special technique needed is increasing (see page 125).

METHOD: This garment is made in one piece, starting at the back hemline. Using 3mm (US 2) needles, cast on 49 (55:61) stitches and work 48 (54:60) rows in garter stitch (every row: slip the first stitch, knit to the end).

SHAPE SLEEVES: Cast on 7 (11:15) stitches at the beginning of the next 2 rows. *63 (77:91) stitches.* Work a further 28 (34:40) rows in garter stitch.

SHAPE NECK: Next row: slip the first stitch, knit 21 (27:33) stitches, cast off 19 (21:23) stitches, knit to end.

SHAPE LEFT FRONT: Working on first set of 22 (28:34) stitches, knit 8 rows, ending at the sleeve edge. **Row 9:** knit to the last 3 stitches, increase in the next stitch, knit 2 stitches. **Row 10:** knit 1 stitch, increase in the next stitch, knit to the end. Repeat rows 9 and 10 until you have 44 (56:68) stitches, ending at the sleeve edge. **Next row:** cast off 7 (11:15) stitches, knit to the last 3 stitches, increase in the next stitch, knit 2 stitches. Continue increasing at the neck edge as before until you have 49 (55:61) stitches. Knit a further 38 (46:54) rows without shaping. Cast off.

SHAPE RIGHT FRONT: Rejoin yarn to remaining 22 (28:34) stitches at the neck edge and knit 8 rows, ending at the neck edge. **Row 9:** knit 1 stitch, increase in the next stitch, knit to the end. **Row 10:** slip the first stitch, knit to the last 3 stitches, increase in the next stitch, knit 2 stitches. Repeat rows 9 and 10 until you have 43 (55:67) stitches, ending at the sleeve edge. **Next row:** cast off 7 (11:15) stitches, knit to the last 3 stitches, increase in the next stitch, knit 2 stitches. Continue increasing at the neck edge as before until you have 49 (55:61) stitches. Knit a further 38 (46:54) rows without shaping. Cast off.

TO FINISH: Weave in all ends, along the fabric not up the side edge. Lay work out flat and gently steam. Cut the length of ribbon in half and sew the ribbon onto each front below the shaped edge. Join left side and sleeve seam. Join right side and sleeve seam, leaving a small opening to match the ribbon position of left front.

TO FASTEN: Cross right front over left front and thread ribbon on left front through opening. Tie at the back.

opposite: This simple kimono-shaped wrap top is knitted in one piece in easy garter stitch. A small hole is left in one side seam just below the armhole for the ribbon to pass through when the vest is wrapped over. The ribbons must be securely tied at the back, out of the baby's reach. Alternatively, secure the kimono with a button and loop fastening.

cashmere teddy bear

This really simple teddy bear is a gift to cherish.

It is constructed like a sweater with a back,

front, sleeves (as arms), and a head knitted in

one piece, and two little ears. The wonderfully

soft yarn makes it an instant favourite for any

baby to cuddle. Once knitted, it is simply

stitched and filled with soft stuffing. A simple

chart (on page 123) shows you where to

increase and decrease. The teddy's face is

embroidered in satin stitch. You can personal-

ize it in any way you choose. A cotton bow

under the chin provides the finishing touch.

top left: This charming first teddy is knitted in four simple pieces (three of them twice).

top right: Once the torso, arms and legs are knitted and sewn together, the head can be sewn together too. The parts are then turned right sides out, and the body and head stuffed and finally sewn together.

right: The face is embroidered onto the teddy with thick black yarn. Sew French knots for the eyes and satin or long stitches for the nose and mouth. To finish, tie a ribbon around the neck.

how to make : cashmere teddy bear

SIZE: Height: 15cm (6in).

MATERIALS: 1 x 50g ball 4 ply yarn, e.g. Jaeger cashmere • Pair of 3^1/$_4$mm (US 3) needles • Black embroidery thread • Safety pin • Ribbon • Filling/stuffing (washable).

TENSION (GAUGE): 26 stitches and 36 rows to 10cm (4in) square measured over stocking (stockinette) stitch using 3^1/$_4$mm (US 3) needles.

TECHNIQUES: The only special techniques required are simple increasing and decreasing, and reading a chart (see page 125).

METHOD: Work in stocking (stockinette) stitch for all pieces. Charts for all parts are on page 123.

FRONT: FIRST LEG: Using 3^1/$_4$mm (US 5) needles, cast on 6 stitches and knit 1 row. Increase 1 stitch at each end of the next 2 rows. ★ **Row 4:** increase 1 stitch at the beginning of the row, purl to the end. Work 3 rows. **Row 8:** purl, increase 1 stitch at the end of the row. *12 stitches.* Work 4 rows. Break yarn and leave the stitches on a safety pin.

SECOND LEG: Work as for first leg to ★. **Row 4:** purl, increase 1 stitch at the end of the row. Work 3 rows. **Row 8:** increase 1 stitch at the beginning of the row, purl to the end. Work 4 rows. **Row 13:** knit 12 stitches, cast on 2 stitches, knit across 12 stitches from first leg.

BODY: Continue in stocking (stockinette) stitch until the work measures 8cm (3^1/$_4$in) from his toes, ending with a purl row. Shape for the arms by decreasing 1 stitch at each end of the next and every following third row until 18 stitches remain. Work 2 more rows. Cast off.

BACK: Work as for front of teddy bear.

THE ARMS: *make 2.* Using 3^1/$_4$mm (US 3) needles, cast on 14 stitches. Knit 1 row. Increase 1 stitch at each end of the next 3 rows. *20 stitches.* Work 11 rows. Decrease 1 stitch at each end of the next 8 rows. Cast off the remaining 4 stitches.

THE EARS: *make 2.* Using 3^1/$_4$mm (US 3) needles, cast on 3 stitches and knit 1 row. Increase 1 stitch at each end of the next 3 rows. *9 stitches.* Work 5 rows. Decrease 1 stitch at each end of the next 3 rows. *3 stitches.* Cast off.

THE HEAD: Using 3^1/$_4$mm (US 5) needles, cast on 36 stitches and work 2 rows. Increase 1 stitch at each end of the next 7 rows. *50 stitches.* Purl 1 row. Decrease 1 stitch at each end of the next 13 rows. *24 stitches.* Purl 1 row. Decrease 1 stitch at each end of the next and every alternate row until 8 stitches remain. Decrease 1 stitch at each end of the next 2 rows. Cast off the remaining 4 stitches.

TO MAKE UP: Lay the pieces out flat, and steam gently. With right sides of the fabric together, sew the sloping end of the arms to the armholes of the 2 body pieces. Leave the neck open. Starting with one arm, using a fine backstitch, sew around "hand", arm, body, both legs and back to the other "hand". Turn right side out. Stuff with filling. Make up head. Pin cast on edge into a circle and B to C (see chart on page 123). Sew seam. Pin point A to seam at BC to make nose. Stitch seam D-nose-D. Turn right side out. Stuff the head. Attach the head to the body, by over-sewing neatly. Mould the head to suit, and characterize. Fold each ear in half, and over sew together. Attach to the head. Embroider 2 eyes with French knots. Embroider the nose in the shape of a triangle, then stitch 2 lines from the base of the nose for the mouth. Finally tie a ribbon around the neck.

vintage cardigan

A classic edge-to-edge cardigan pattern in stocking (stockinette) stitch finds a
new lease of life knitted in 4-ply botany wool with an attractive velvet ribbon
trim, bordering the neck, fronts and hem. Simple roll back cuffs add a practical
finishing touch, allowing room for the baby to grow. Make it in muted art
shades, like the soft violet colour shown here.

how to make: vintage cardigan

SIZING: For sizing refer to chart on page 114.

MATERIALS: 3 (3:3) x 50g balls Rowan true 4 ply botany wool • Pair of 3¼mm (US 3) needles • 3 safety pins • Sewing needle • Velvet ribbon, approximately 110 (120:130)cm, 43 (47:50)in, long, or trim of choice.

TENSION (GAUGE): 28 stitches and 36 rows to 10cm (4in) square over stocking (stockinette) stitch using 3¼mm (US 3) needles.

TECHNIQUES: Simple increasing and decreasing are the only special techniques needed for this pattern (see explanation on page l25).

METHOD: BACK: Using 3¼mm (US 3) needles, cast on 67 (75:83) stitches and knit 3 rows. Right side of work facing, change to stocking (stockinette) stitch and continue until work measures 13 (15:16)cm, 5 (6:6½)in.

SHAPE ARMHOLES: Cast off 4 stitches at the beginning of the next 2 rows. Decrease 1 stitch at each end of the next 6 rows. *47 (55:63) stitches.* Continue until work measures 20 (23:26)cm, 8 (9:10)in. Cast off 12 (15:18) stitches at the beginning of the next 2 rows. Break yarn and slip remaining 23 (25:27) stitches onto a safety pin.

RIGHT FRONT: Using 3¼mm (US 3) needles, cast on 34 (38:42) stitches and knit 3 rows. Right side of work facing, change to stocking (stockinette) stitch with garter stitch edge as follows: **Row 1:** knit. **Row 2:** purl to last 3 stitches, knit 3 stitches. Repeat these 2 rows until work measures 13 (15:16)cm, 5 (6:6½)in, ending with row 1.

SHAPE ARMHOLE: Cast off 4 stitches, purl to last 3 stitches,knit 3 stitches. Decrease 1 stitch at armhole edge on the next 6 rows. *24 (28:32) stitches.* Then continue, without shaping, until the work measures 18 (20:22)cm, 7 (7¾:8¾)in, ending with a knit row.

SHAPE NECK: Purl to last 6 (7:8) stitches, then slip these 6 (7:8) stitches onto a safety pin. Continue in stocking (stockinette) stitch, decreasing 1 stitch at the neck edge on the next 6 rows. *12 (15:18) stitches.* Continue until

work measures 20 (23:26)cm, 8 (9:10)in, ending with a purl row. Cast off.

LEFT FRONT: Using $3^1/_4$mm (US 3) needles, cast on 34 (38:42) stitches and knit 3 rows. Right side of work facing, change to stocking (stockinette) stitch with garter stitch edge as follows: **Row 1:** knit. **Row 2:** knit 3 stitches, purl to the end of the row. Repeat these 2 rows until the work measures 13 (15:16)cm, 5 (6:6$^1/_2$)in, ending with row 2.

SHAPE ARMHOLE: Cast off 4 stitches, knit to end of row. Decrease 1 stitch at armhole edge on the next 6 rows. *24 (28:32) stitches.* Continue without shaping until work measures 18 (20:22)cm, 7 (7$^3/_4$:8$^3/_4$)in, ending with a purl row.

SHAPE NECK: Knit to last 6 (7:8) stitches and then slip these 6 (7:8) stitches onto a safety pin. Continue in stocking (stockinette) stitch, decreasing 1 stitch at neck edge on the next 6 rows. *12 (15:18) stitches.* Continue until work measures 20 (23:26)cm, 8 (9:10)in, ending with a purl row. Cast off.

NECKBAND: Sew shoulder seams. With right side facing, join yarn to the right front edge and knit across 6 (7:8) stitches on the safety pin, pick up and knit 12

opposite: You may wish to make little slippers to co-ordinate with the vintage style cardigan. These ones are knitted in fine wool and trimmed in the same decorative ribbon. Refer to the instructions for the silk slippers (page 82) and simply change the yarn.

(14:14) stitches to the shoulder, knit across 23 (25:27) stitches of the back neck, pick up and knit 12 (14:14) stitches down to the left front edge and knit across the last 6 (7:8)stitches on safety pin. *59 (65:71) stitches.* Knit 2 rows. Cast off.

SLEEVES: Using $3^1/_4$mm (US 3) needles, cast on 36 (36:40) stitches and work in garter stitch for 4 (4:5)cm, 1$^1/_2$ (1$^1/_2$:2)in. Change to stocking (stockinette) stitch, increasing 1 stitch at each end of every 6th row, until the sleeve measures 14 (17:19)cm, 5$^1/_2$ (6$^1/_2$:7$^1/_2$)in.

SHAPE SLEEVEHEAD: Knit 2 stitches together at the beginning of the next 10 rows. Cast off.

TO FINISH: Sew in any loose ends. Lay the work out flat, pin out pieces and gently steam. Sew the sleeveheads into the armholes between shapings. Sew the side and sleeve seams. Turn up cuff.

TO DECORATE: Starting at the right side seam, pin the ribbon above the garter stitch hem, across the bottom of the back and left front; up the left front, around the neck, down the right front and across the front to the side seam. Sew into position with fine stitches.

sssh! baby sleeping cushion

This little cushion can be used to hang on the nursery or bedroom door to warn the household that the baby is asleep and must not be disturbed. One of the easiest projects in the book to make, it is an ideal gift for a first baby. It is knitted here in silk but could easily be made from cotton. The two little stocking (stockinette) stitch squares are simply stitched together and stuffed. The front is embroidered in cross stitch (see chart on page 123), Embroider the words and add an X for a loving kiss, or, if you prefer, embroider the baby's name or initials.

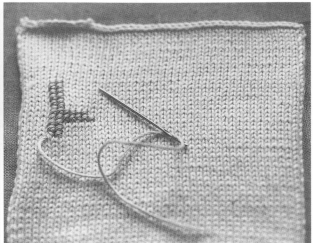

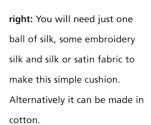

right: You will need just one ball of silk, some embroidery silk and silk or satin fabric to make this simple cushion. Alternatively it can be made in cotton.

how to make: sssh! baby sleeping cushion

above right: Follow the chart given on page 123 to work the embroidery as shown, or personalize it with the baby's name or a little message of your choice.

opposite: A simple gift for a baby shower, this little cushion can be embroidered in pink or blue, to be hung on the nursery door to warn others not to disturb the baby while she or he is sleeping.

SIZE: This cushion measures approximately 13cm (5in) square.

MATERIALS: 1 x 50g ball fine yarn, e.g Jaeger 4 ply silk or Jaeger Siena cotton • Pair of 2mm (US 1) needles • Embroidery thread • Silk or synthetic ribbon, approximately 1m (39in) long x 1cm ($^1/_2$in) wide • Sewing needle • Silk or satin fabric, measuring approximately 15cm x 28cm (6in x 11in), for the cushion • Suitable stuffing for the cushion.

TENSION (GAUGE): 36 stitches and 46 rows to 10cm (4in) square measured over stocking (stockinette) stitch using 2mm (US 1) needles.

TECHNIQUES: Slip the first stitch and knit the last stitch of every row to give a neat edge. You will need to refer to the chart on page 117.

METHOD: Using 2mm (US 1) needles, cast on 44

stitches and work in stocking (stockinette) stitch for 56 rows. Cast off. Make a second piece to match.

TO EMBROIDER: Follow the chart given on page 123. Work in cross stitch.

TO MAKE UP: Lay the work out flat and press gently on the wrong side. Sew three sides.

TO MAKE THE PAD: Fold the fabric in half lengthways and sew the 2 side seams. Turn it right sides out and then stuff with filling and sew up the remaining edge. Insert the pad into the knitted square, and carefully sew the remaining seam.

TO FINISH: Cut a 36cm (14in) length of the ribbon. Attach this length of ribbon as a handle to the top of the cushion from the left corner to the right corner. Cut the remaining length of ribbon in half and tie into 2 bows and sew one to each top corner of the cushion.

lace-edged cuddle blanket

This classic baby blanket can be used in the pram, the cot or the car. Whether you knit it in white or in soft washed pastel shades, it is a timeless classic that will probably be handed down from baby to baby. Although it takes a little time to knit, the blanket is easy because it is knitted in sections made from stocking (stockinette) stitch and reverse stocking (stockinette) stitch, while the lace edging is knitted in four strips that are then joined together to edge the blanket. This particular blanket was knitted in cool natural cotton, but a warmer blanket could be worked in soft, luxurious merino wool.

how to make: **lace-edged cuddle blanket**

SIZE: This blanket measures approximately 110 cm (43³/₄in) square.

MATERIALS: 17 x 50g balls fine cotton, e.g. Rowan Cotton Glace • Pair of 3¹/₄mm (US 3) needles • Sewing needle

TENSION (GAUGE): 23 stitches and 32 rows to 10cm (4in) square measured over stocking (stockinette) stitch using 3¹/₄mm (US 3) needles.

TECHNIQUES: Slip the first and knit the last stitch of every row to give a firm edge. "Yarn round needle" means bring yarn to the front of work (as if to purl a stitch) and take over the needle to the back, so making a stitch. "Yarn twice round needle" means bring yarn to the front of work, wind around needle twice, so making 2 stitches.

METHOD: Using 3¹/₄mm (US 3) needles, cast on 60 stitches and work in stocking (stockinette) stitch until work measures 26cm, (10¹/₄in), approximately 84 rows. Cast off. This makes one square. Make a total of 16 squares.

TO MAKE UP: Sew in all ends by weaving along the knitting not along the edge. Lay each square out flat and gently steam. Next lay out the 16 squares in a grid of 4 squares wide by 4 squares deep, alternating right and wrong sides to make a pattern. Pin the squares together and oversew the edges.

LACE EDGING: This edging is worked lengthwise. Due to the nature of the pattern the number of stitches varies on some rows.
Using 3¹/₄mm (US 3) needles, cast on 10 stitches. Work as follows: **Row 1:** (right side) knit 3 stitches, ★ yarn round needle, knit 2 stitches together ★. Repeat ★ to ★, yarn twice round needle, knit 2 stitches together, knit 1 stitch *11 stitches.* **Row 2:** knit 3 stitches, purl 1 stitch, knit 2 stitches, ★ yarn round needle, knit 2 stitches together ★. Repeat ★ to ★, knit 1 stitch. **Row 3:** knit 3 stitches, ★ yarn round needle, knit 2 stitches together ★. Repeat ★ to ★, knit 1 stitch, yarn twice round needle, knit 2 stitches together, knit 1 stitch. *12 stitches.* **Row 4:** knit 3 stitches, purl 1 stitch, knit 3 stitches, ★ yarn round needle, knit 2 stitches together ★. Repeat ★ to ★, knit 1 stitch. **Row 5:** knit 3 stitches, ★ yarn round needle, knit 2 stitches together ★. Repeat ★ to ★, knit 2 stitches, yarn twice round needle, knit 2 stitches together, knit 1 stitch *13 stitches.* **Row 6:** knit 3 stitches, purl 1 stitch, knit 4 stitches, ★ yarn round needle, knit 2 stitches together ★. Repeat ★ to ★, knit 1 stitch. **Row 7:** knit 3 stitches, ★ yarn round needle, knit 2 stitches together ★. Repeat ★ to ★, knit 6 stitches. **Row 8:** cast off 3 stitches, knit 5 stitches (1 stitch already on right needle) ★ yarn round needle, knit 2 stitches together ★. Repeat ★ to ★, knit 1 stitch. *10 stitches.* Repeat these 8 rows until work, when slightly stretched, measures 110cm (43¹/₄in), ending with row 8. Cast off. Make 4 strips of lace in total.

TO FINISH: Sew in all ends by weaving along the knitting, not up the side. Pin a strip of lace edging to one side of the blanket so that the strip extends 3cm (1¼in) over one end. Pin the second strip in place all along next side, sewing one end to overlap and letting strip extend 3cm (1¼in) over other end. Sew on third and fourth strips in the same way. Taking care to ease corners to continue the scallop effect, lay work out flat and steam gently.

opposite left: Alternate the right and wrong sides of the knitted squares to make a patchwork effect .

opposite centre: Pin a strip of lace edging all along one side of the blanket, easing it as you do, and extending it over the corner of the blanket. Then sew into position.

opposite right: The second, third and fourth strips are sewn in the same way,

left: The finished lace-edged blanket .

garter stitch silk slippers

Knitted in the very simplest garter stitch in fine silk, these delicate little slippers are the ideal gift for a new born baby, particularly when decorated with a rosebud trim or matching organza ribbons. Soft, stretchy and snug, they can be knitted in three sizes for babies from birth to nine months old. Only very simple shaping is needed, and the slippers can be knitted up in a few hours.

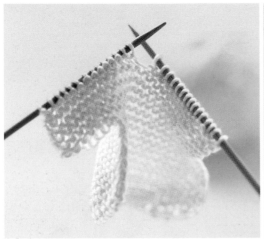

how to make: **garter stitch silk slippers**

SIZING: For sizing refer to chart on page 114.

MATERIALS: 1 x 50g ball 4 ply silk, eg Jaeger 4 ply silk • Pair of $2^3/_4$mm (US 2) needles • Sewing needle • Organza ribbon 1cm ($^1/_2$in) wide x 124cm (49in) long

TENSION (GAUGE): 28 stitches and 38 rows to 10cm square measured over garter stitch using $2^3/_4$mm (US 2) needles.

TECHNIQUES: Only simple increasing and decreasing are needed for this pattern (see explanation on page 125).

METHOD: Using $2^3/_4$mm (US 2) needles cast on 12 (16:20) stitches and work in garter stitch, every row knit. Increase 1 stitch at each end of the first and every alternate row until 24 (28:32) stitches are on the needle. Knit 2 rows without shaping. Decrease 1 stitch at each end of the first and every following alternate row until

above left: Each slipper is knitted in one piece, with very simple shaping.

above centre: The finished slipper before being stitched up.

above right: The untrimmed slippers, showing the simple shape used. When making up each slipper, sew the heel seam first and then join the sole to the upper, easing in any fullness.

opposite: Matching organza ribbon is stitched to the slippers at the heel seam as a finishing touch.

12 (16:20) stitches remain. You have now knitted the sole of the slipper. Cast on 7 stitches for the heel at the end of the last row. *19 (23:27) stitches*. Continue on these stitches, keeping the heel edge straight, increasing 1 stitch at the toe edge on every alternate row until there are 25 (29:33) stitches on the needle, ending at heel edge. Cast off 12 (15:18) stitches at the heel, knit to the end. Knit 13 (15:17) rows. Cast on 12 (15:18) stitches at the (heel) end of the last row. *25 (29:33) stitches*. Keeping the heel edge straight decrease 1 stitch at the toe edge on every alternate row until 19 (23:27) stitches remain. Cast off.

TO FINISH: Sew in any loose ends. Join the straight seam at heel. Join the sole to the top of the slipper, easing the fullness around the toe. Cut length of ribbon in half. Then fold one length of the organza ribbon in half and sew it to the centre back of the slipper. Alternatively, personalize with embellishment of your choice.

traditional mabel dress

This delightful dress for a small girl has nostalgic appeal, particularly if knitted in dusty pink or soft mauve. Worked in stocking (stockinette) stitch, the dress is gathered onto a simple yolk with a tiny picot edging detail at the neck. Knit it in soft fine cotton for summer, or in cashmere for winter. Fine organza ribbon ties the back of the dress at the neck, with a simple centre slit opening that slides easily over the baby's head. A simple garter stitch hem gives body to the base of the skirt.

how to make: traditional mabel dress

right: This simple little dress, with its yoke and decorative picot edging, is worked in fine 4 ply mercerized cotton, which gives an attractive sheen and a touch of nostalgia to this timeless design

SIZING: For sizing refer to chart on page 115.

MATERIALS: 3 (3:4) x 50g balls fine yarn e.g. Jaeger Siena 100% mercerized cotton • 2 pairs of $2^3/_4$mm (US 2) needles • Pair of $2^1/_4$mm (US 1) needles • Ribbon, approximately 84cm (33in) long and 1cm ($^1/_2$in) wide • Sewing needle

TENSION (GAUGE): 30 stitches and 38 rows to 10cm (4in) square measured over stocking (stockinette) stitch using $2^3/_4$mm (US 2) needles.

TECHNIQUES: Just a few special techniques are needed. Increasing and decreasing, knitting through the back of the loops and making a stitch without leaving a hole (up 1 stitch). See page 125 for explanations.

METHOD: BACK: Using $2^3/_4$mm (US 2) needles, cast on 125 (131:137) stitches and work 5 rows in garter stitch, every row: knit.
Change to stocking (stockinette) stitch and continue until work measures 19 (22:25)cm, $7^1/_2$ ($8^3/_4$:10)in, ending with a purl row.

BACK OPENING: Next row: knit 62 (65:68) stitches, cast off 1 stitch, knit 62 (65:68) stitches. Now work on the second set of stitches, knitting the last stitch of all purl rows to give a neat edge to the back opening. Continue in stocking (stockinette) stitch until work measures 22 (25:28)cm, $8^1/_2$ (10:11)in, ending with a knit row.

SHAPE ARMHOLE: Row 1: cast off 2 stitches, purl to the last stitch, knit 1 stitch. **Row 2:** knit to the last 4 stitches, knit 2 stitches together through the back loops, knit 2 stitches. **Row 3:** purl to the last stitch knit 1 stitch. Repeat rows 2 and 3 three times. *56 (59:62) stitches.* **★★ Decrease row:** knit 2 stitches together 28 (29:31) times, knit 0 (1:0) stitch. *28 (30:31) stitches.* Knit 3 rows to mark back yoke. Continue in stocking (stockinette) stitch until work measures 31 (35:39)cm, $12^1/_4$ ($13^3/_4$:$15^1/_4$)in, ending with a purl row. **★★**

SHAPE NECK: Row 1: cast off 10 (11:11) stitches, knit to end. **Row 2:** purl. **Row 3:** cast off 4 stitches, knit to end. Work 2 rows without shaping. Cast off.
With wrong side of work facing, rejoin yarn to remaining 62 (65:68) stitches at

opening edge, knit 1 stitch, purl to end. Continue in stocking (stockinette) stitch until work measures 22 (25:28)cm, 8¹/₂ (10:11)in, ending with a purl row.

SHAPE ARMHOLE: **Row 1:** cast off 2 stitches, knit to end. **Row 2:** knit 1 stitch, purl to end. **Row 3:** knit 2 stitches, knit 2 stitches together, knit to end. **Row 4:** knit 1 stitch, purl to end. Repeat rows 3 and 4 three times. *56 (59:62) stitches.* Work from ★★ to ★★ as on first side but end with a knit row (work 1 row less).

SHAPE NECK: **Row 1:** cast of 10 (11:11) stitches, purl to end. **Row 2:** knit. **Row 3:** cast off 4 stitches, purl to end. Work 3 more rows without shaping. Cast off.

FRONT: Cast on and garter stitch border as for back. Change to stocking (stockinette) stitch and continue until work measures 22 (25:28)cm, 8¹/₂ (10:11)in, ending with a purl row.

above left: The sleeves are gently shaped by working simple decreases that give a fully-fashioned effect and trimmed with a simple rib stitch cuff.

above right: A picot edge is a simple yet pretty way to finish an otherwise plain neckline. It is an easy stitch yet very effective.

SHAPE ARMHOLE: **Rows 1 and 2:** cast off 2 stitches at the beginning of each row, work to end. **Row 3:** knit 2 stitches, knit 2 stitches together, knit to the last 4 stitches, knit 2 stitches together through the back loops, knit 2 stitches. **Row 4:** purl. Repeat rows 3 and 4 three times. *113 (119:125) stitches.* **Decrease row:** ★ knit 2 stitches together 55 (58:61) times, knit 3 stitches together. *56 (59:62) stitches.* Knit 3 rows to mark the front yoke. Continue in stocking (stockinette) stitch until work measures 29 (33:37)cm, 11¹/₂ (13:14¹/₂)in, ending with a purl row.

SHAPE NECK: **Next row:** knit 21 (22:23) stitches, cast off 14 (15:16) stitches, knit 21 (22:23) stitches. Now work on the second set of 21 (22:23) stitches. ★★ Decrease 1 stitch at the neck on the next 7 rows. Work 4 rows. Cast off. ★★ With wrong side of work facing, rejoin yarn to the remaining 21 (22:23) stitches at the neck edge and work from ★★ to ★★ again.

SLEEVES: *make 2 the same.* With 2¹/₄mm (US 1) needles, cast on 47 (51:55) stitches and work 5 (7:7) rows in rib

as follows: **Row 1:** ★ knit 1 stitch, purl 1 stitch, repeat from ★ to the last stitch, knit 1 stitch. **Row 2:** ★ purl 1 stitch, knit 1 stitch, repeat from ★ to the last stitch, purl 1 stitch. Repeat rows 1 and 2 once (twice:twice) more, then row 1 again.

Increase row: rib 1 (3:5) stitches, ★ up 1 stitch, rib 5 stitches, repeat from ★ to last 1 (3:5) stitches, up 1 stitch, rib 1 (3:5) stitches. *57 (61:65) stitches.* Change to 2³/₄mm (US 2) needles and work in stocking (stockinette) stitch. Increase 1 stitch at each end of the third row and every following alternate row until there are 67 (71:75) stitches. Work 3 more rows.

SHAPE SLEEVEHEAD: **Rows 1 and 2:** cast off 2 stitches at the beginning of each row, work to end. **Row 3:** knit 2 stitches, knit 2 stitches together, knit to the last 4 stitches, knit 2 stitches together through the back loops, knit 2 stitches. **Row 4:** purl. Repeat rows 3 and 4 three times. *55 (59:63) stitches.* **Decrease row:** knit 2 (1:1) stitches ★ knit 2 stitches together, knit 4 stitches, repeat from ★ to last 5 (4:2) stitches, knit 2 stitches togther, knit 3 (2:0) stitches. **Next row:** knit. Cast off.

NECKTRIM: Join shoulder seams. With right side of garment facing and using 2³/₄mm (US 2) needles, pick up and knit 14 (15:16) stitches from back opening to shoulder seam, 10 stitches down front neck, 14 (15:16) stitches from centre front neck, 10 stitches up front side neck and 14 (15:16) stitches from shoulder seam to back opening. *62 (65:68) stitches.* Knit 1 row.

To work picot edge, cast off 3 stitches ★ slip the stitch on the right needle back on to the left needle, cast on 2 stitches, cast off 5 stitches. Repeat from ★ to the end of the row. Cast off the last stitch.

TO MAKE UP: Weave in all the loose ends. Lay work out flat and gently steam, ease in the sleeves between the armhole shaping, the straight edge of the sleeve fitting between the yokes, and the sloping edge attached to the body of the dress. Stitch into position. Join side and sleeve seams.

TO FINISH: Cut the length of ribbon in half and attach each piece securely to either side of the top of the back centre opening.

left: It is often difficult to get a wriggling baby in and out of its clothes. This dress has no fiddly buttons, the back being fastened simply with a ribbon tie, attached to either side of the back neck opening.

ribbon-tied wool vest

Another classic straight from the family photograph album, this little ribbon-edged vest is a brilliant gift for a new born baby. Knit it in classic white, or in soft blue, taupe or grey in merino or botany wool for extra winter warmth. Slot fine silk ribbon through the eyelets in the neck band, tied in a bow at the centre to create the finishing detail. The shoulder seams are grafted together for a smooth finish, ensuring that the baby's soft skin is not irritated.

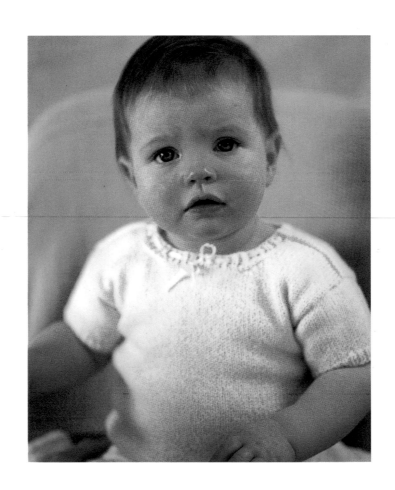

how to make: ribbon-tied wool vest

above left: This design is
best knitted in fine yarn,
merino wool or cotton is the
preferred choice for its natural
qualities and ultimate
comfort.

above centre: Simple eyelets
are worked around the neck
and threaded with fine silk
(or possibly velvet) and tied in
a bow. The fully fashioned
detail at the neck edge gives
an authentic touch to this
classic garment.

SIZING: For sizing refer to chart on page 115.

MATERIALS: 2 (2:2) x 50g balls fine wool, e.g. Rowan true 4 ply botany yarn, Jaeger baby merino or Jaeger matchmaker 4 ply merino • Pair of 3mm (US 2) needles • Pair of $3^{1}/_{4}$mm (US 3) needles, plus spare • 6 x safety pins • Sewing needle • Silk ribbon, 4mm ($^{1}/_{4}$in) wide and approximately 65cm (26 in) long

TENSION (GAUGE): 28 stitches and 36 rows to 10cm (4in) square measured over stocking (stockinette) stitch using $3^{1}/_{4}$mm (US 3) needles.

TECHNIQUES: Simple increases and decreases and bringing yarn forward to make an eyelet (see page 125).

METHOD: BACK: Using 3mm (US 2) needles, cast on 56 (62:68) stitches. Work 4 (4:6) rows in knit 1, purl 1 rib, every row: ★ knit 1 stitch, purl 1 stitch, repeat from ★ to end. Change to $3^{1}/_{4}$mm (US 3) needles and work in stocking (stockinette) stitch until the knitting measures 13.5 (15:16.5)cm, $5^{1}/_{4}$ ($6:6^{1}/_{2}$)in. Tie a coloured thread to each end of the next row to mark the armhole. Continue knitting until the work measures 16.5 (19:21.5)cm, $6^{1}/_{2}$ ($7^{1}/_{2}:8^{1}/_{4}$)in, ending with a purl row.

above right: Simply shaped sleeves are set into the body. The shoulders are "grafted" together to give a flat appearance, with no bulky inside seams.

opposite: If you start in plenty of time for the baby's birth, you can knit several of these little vests and store them in a tiny linen basket to await the new arrival.

SHAPE NECK: Knit 22 (24:26) stitches, turn and work on these stitches as follows: ★ Decrease 1 stitch at the neck edge on every row until 14 (16:18) stitches remain. Continue until work measures 21.5 (24:26.5)cm, $8^1/_2$ ($9^1/_2$:$10^1/_2$)in. Break yarn and leave these stitches on a safety pin. ★ Slip the centre 12 (14:16) stitches onto a safety pin. With right side facing, rejoin the yarn to the remaining 22 (24:26) stitches at the neck edge and knit to the end of the row. Then work from ★ to ★ as on the first side.

FRONT: Work as for back.

SLEEVES: *make 2 the same.* Using 3mm (US 2) needles, cast on 46 (50:54) stitches and work 4 rows in knit 1, purl 1 rib as on back.
Change to $3^1/_4$mm (US 3) needles and work in stocking (stockinette) stitch for 2 (2.5:3)cm, $^3/_4$ (1:$1^1/_4$)in.

SHAPE SLEEVEHEAD: Decrease 1 stitch at the beginning of the next 10 rows. Cast off.

TO MAKE UP: Place 14 (16:18) right shoulder stitches onto $3^1/_4$mm (US 3) needles

GRAFT SHOULDER SEAM: Hold the two needles with equal number of shoulder stitches on together, with the fabric wrong sides of the knitting facing each other, in the left hand. Using spare needle, place the point of the right needle through the first stitch of the front and the back needle and knit together, do the same to the next two stitches on the left needles, and then cast off by pulling second stitch on right needle over first stitch on right needle. Continue like this along the row until all the stitches have been cast off. This will form a detail ridge row on the right side of the fabric.

NECKTRIM: Using 3mm (US 2) needles and with the right side of the work facing you, pick up and knit 14 (15:16) stitches along the left front side neck, 12 (14:16) stitches from the safety pin, 14 (15:16) stitches along the right front side neck to the shoulder, 14 (15:16) stitches down back right side neck, 12 (14:16) stitches from the safety pin and finally 14 (15:16) stitches from along the left back side neck. *80 (88:96) stitches.* **Row 1:** purl 1 stitch, knit 1 stitch, alternately to the end of the row.

MAKE EYELETS: Row 2: ★ purl 1 stitch, knit 1 stitch, yarn forward, knit 2 stitches together, repeat from ★ to the end. **Row 3:** purl 1 stitch, knit 1 stitch alternately to the end of the row. **Row 4:** cast off in rib as set.

TO FINISH: Graft the other shoulder seam. Weave in all ends along the work, not up the sides. Lay work out flat and gently steam. Set sleeveheads between the coloured threads and stitch. Join side and sleeve seams. Join necktrim at shoulder. Thread the ribbon through the eyelets and tie at centre front.

opposite: This vintage-style vest, knitted in soft fine merino wool or light cool cotton, cossets the baby as the natural fibres allow the body to breathe, while keeping the baby comfortable.

rosebud cardigan

An ideal gift for a special occasion, this pretty stocking (stockinette) stitch cardigan is knitted in silk or mercerized cotton. The pearly sheen of the yarn is emphasized with a delicate rosebud trim or mother-of-pearl buttons. The front neck band is knitted integrally, giving it a very neat finish. Knit it up in bronze or grey for a small boy, without the rosebud trim. The decreasing stitches on the raglan shoulders are knitted two stitches in from the edge to create an attractive fully fashioned detail and a neater edge for sewing up.

how to make: rosebud cardigan

SIZING: For sizing refer to chart on page 115.

MATERIALS: 2 (2:3) x 50g balls of fine yarn, e.g. Jaeger 4 ply silk or Jaeger 4 ply Siena cotton • Pair of 2^3/$_4$mm (US 2) needles • Pair of 2^1/$_4$mm • (US 1) needles • Sewing needle • 4 rosebuds or buttons.

TENSION (GAUGE): 30 stitches and 38 rows to 10cm (4in) square measured over stocking (stockinette) stitch using 2^3/$_4$mm (US 2) needles.

TECHNIQUES: Work the cast on edge with a size smaller needle to neaten the edge. For this pattern, you also need to be able to work increases and decreases, make eyelets, knit through the back of the loops and pick up stitches (see page 125 for explanations).

METHOD: BACK: Using 2^3/$_4$mm (US 2) needles cast on 68 (76:84) stitches and work 6 rows in garter stitch, every row knit. Change to stocking (stockinette) stitch and work 34 (40:48) rows.

SHAPE RAGLAN ARMHOLE: Cast off 3 (3:2) stitches at the beginning of the next two rows. Work fully fashioned detail as follows. **Row 1:** knit 1 stitch, knit next 2 stitches together, knit to last 3 stitches, knit next 2 stitches together through the back loops, knit the last stitch. **Row 2:** purl. Repeat rows 1 and 2 until 28 (30:32) stitches remain. Cast off.

LEFT FRONT: Using 2^3/$_4$mm (US 2) needles, cast on 36 (40:44) stitches and work 6 rows in garter stitch, every row knit. Change to stocking (stockinette) stitch with garter stitch button band as follows: **Row 1:** knit across row. **Row 2:** knit 4 stitches, purl to end. Repeat rows 1 and 2 16 (19:23) times. *34 (40:48) rows.*

SHAPE RAGLAN ARMHOLE: Row 1: cast off 3 (3:2) stitches, knit to end. **Row 2:** knit 4 stitches, purl to end. **Row 3:** knit 1 stitch, knit 2 stitches together, knit to end. **Row 4:** knit 4 stitches, purl to end. Repeat rows 3 and 4 until 21 (22:23) stitches remain, ending with row 3.

SHAPE NECK: Cast off 7 (8:9) stiches, purl to end. Now decrease 1 stitch at each end of every row until 2 stitches remain. Knit 2 stitches together. Fasten off.

RIGHT FRONT: Using 2^3/$_4$mm (US 2) needles, cast on 36 (40:44) stitches and work 6 rows in garter stitch. Change to stocking (stockinette) stitch with garter stitch buttonhole band as follows: **Row 1:** knit across row. **Row 2:** purl to last 4 stitches, knit 4 stitches.

WORK THE FIRST BUTTONHOLE: Row 3: knit 2 stitches, yarn forward, knit 2 stitches together, knit to the end. Work 32 (38:46) more rows. *35 (41:49) rows,* making second buttonhole (as row 3) on row 23 (27:33).

SHAPE RAGLAN ARMHOLE (WRONG SIDE FACING): Row 1: cast off 3 (3:2) stitches, purl to last 4 stitches, knit 4 stitches. **Row 2:** knit to last 3 stitches, knit next 2 stitches together through the back loops, knit 1 stitch. **Row 3:** purl to last 4 stitches, knit 4 stitches. Repeat rows 2 and 3 until 28 (31:35) stitches remain, ending

with row 3. **Next row:** make buttonhole: knit 2 stitches, yarn forward, knit 2 stitches together, knit to last 3 stitches, knit next 2 stitches through the back loops, knit 1 stitch. Continue raglan shaping until 22 (23:24) stitches remain, ending with a purl row.

SHAPE NECK: Cast off 7 (8:9) stitches, knit to last 3 stitches, knit next 2 stitches together through the back loops, knit 1 stitch. **Next row:** purl across row. Decrease 1 stitch at each end of every row until 2 stitches remain. Knit 2 stitches together. Fasten off.

LEFT SLEEVE: Using 2³/₄mm (US 2) needles cast on 36 (42:48) stitches and work 6 rows in garter stitch, every row knit. Change to stocking (stockinette) stitch.

above left: The garter stitch button and buttonhole bands are knitted at the same time as the fronts, this gives a much neater appearance and less sewing up! Decorative rosebuds are used in place of conventional buttons.

above right: Work the decrease stitches for the raglan shaping 2 stitches in from the edge to give a fully-fashioned detail and a neater edge for sewing up.

Increase each end of first and every following 4th row to 52 (60:68) stitches. Continue without shaping until work measures 10 (13:16)cm, 4 (5:6)in, ending with a purl row.

SHAPE RAGLAN ARMHOLE: Cast off 3 (3:2) stitches at the beginning of the next 2 rows. Decrease 1 stitch, fully fashioned, as on back, at each end of the next and every following alternate row until 22 (24:26) stitches remain, ending with a purl row. Now decrease 1 stitch at each end of every row until 8 (10:12) stitches remain, ending with a knit row. Cast off 3 (4:5) stitches, purl to the last 3 stitches, purl 2 stitches together, purl 1 stitch.
Next row: knit 1 stitch, knit 2 stitches together, knit to end. Cast off.

RIGHT SLEEVE: Work as for the left sleeve until 10 (12:14) stitches remain, ending with a purl row. Cast off 3 (4:5) stitches, knit to the last 3 stitches, knit 2 stitches together through the back of loops, knit 1 stitch. **Next row:** Purl 1 stitch, purl 2 stitches together through the back loops, purl 1 (2:3) stitches, purl 2 stitches together. Cast off.

TO MAKE UP: Weave in all ends. Lay work flat, pin down if necessary. Gently steam. Sew front and back raglan seams, with the highest point of sleeve, towards the back. Sew the sleeve and side seams.

NECKBAND: With 2³/₄mm (US 2) needles and with the right side of the work facing you, pick up and knit 13 (14:15) stitches from right front neck, 6 (7:8) stitches across top of right sleeve, 28 (30:32) stitches across the back neck, 6 (7:8) stitches across top of left sleeve, 13 (14:15) stitches from left front neck. *66 (72:78) stitches.* Work 3 rows in garter stitch, making a buttonhole on the first row, as follows: knit to last 4 stitches, knit 2 stitches together, yarn forward, knit 2 stitches. Change to 2¹/₄mm (US 1) needles and knit 1 more row. Cast off.

TO FINISH: Sew up the side and sleeve seams. Attach rosebuds or buttons of your choice to match the buttonholes.

above: A simple raglan sleeve, round-neck style updated in luxurious silk creates a traditional baby cardigan with a twist. Silk takes colour beautifully, so you will be tempted to knit this design over and over again in different colours as gifts for the new arrivals of friends and family.

simple lavender bag

One of the best soporofic herbs, lavender is the ideal stuffing for a simple bag to tuck under the baby's pillow or to hang from the closet door, to scent the baby's room. Knitted in one piece in stocking (stockinette) stitch, with a fine picot edge at the opening, the bag is tied with fine silk ribbon. If you are giving the lavender bag as a present, tie a small silver charm to the ribbon.

how to make: **simple lavender bag**

SIZE: This bag measures 12 x 16cm (4³/₄ x 6¹/₄in)

MATERIALS: 1 x 25g ball of fine silk yarn, e.g. Jaeger 4 ply silk • Pair of 2mm (US 1) needles • Sewing needle • Fine ribbon to trim • Thin muslin, silk or fine cotton fabric for sachet.

TENSION (GAUGE): 36 stitches and 46 rows to 10cm (4in) square measured over stocking (stockinette) stitch using 2mm (US 1) needles.

TECHNIQUES: Bringing yarn forward to make an eyelet through which ribbon is threaded (see page l25 for explanation).

METHOD: Using 2mm (US 1) needles, cast on 83 stitches· and work 12cm (4³/₄in) in stocking (stockinette) stitch, ending with a purl row.

MAKE EYELETS: Knit 5 stitches, ★ yarn forward, knit 2 stitches together, knit 8 stitches, repeat from ★, ending last repeat, knit 6 stitches. Work for another

above left: Fold the finished knitting in half widthways; with the picot edge at the top, and sew along the side and bottom edges.

above centre: A little sachet, filled with lavender seed-heads, is inserted into the finished knitted bag .

above right: Thread fine silk ribbon through the eyelets at the top of the knitted bag, draw it up and fasten it with a decorative bow.

opposite: Lavender has long been recognized as conducive to restful sleep, so place it in the baby's bedding or put it under your own pillow!

3cm (1¹/₄in) in stocking (stockinette) stitch, ending with a purl row.

PICOT EDGE: Cast off 3 stitches, ★ slip the stitch on the right needle back on to the left needle, cast on 2 stitches, cast off 5 stitches. Repeat from ★ to the end of the row. Cast off the last stitch.

TO MAKE UP: Lay the knitting out flat and gently steam. With the right sides of the knitting together, fold the work in half widthways, with the picot edge at the top. Sew along the side and bottom edge. Thread ribbon through the eyelets.

LAVENDER SACHET: Cut a rectangle 12cm (4³/₄in) wide x 26cm (10¹/₄in) deep of the fabric. Fold in half lengthwise and sew the two side seams, leaving the top open. Fill bag with lavender seeds. Turn the top edge over and sew up securely.

TO FINISH: Put lavender sachet into knitted bag. Pull up ribbon and tie in a decorative bow at the front.

106

finishing **touches**

above left: When you fold the garments or knited projects, insert tissue paper between the layers to prevent creasing.

above centre: Metallic paper, finished with gauze ribbon, makes a neat package for a small present.

above right: For a modern touch, wrap up the gift in brown paper, tie it with string and add a small present, like this wooden rattle, with the gift tag.

opposite: Knitted gifts on their way to a baby shower.

IF YOU GO to the trouble of knitting for a new baby, then make sure that you finish off your knitted gift appropriately. Take time and care with the finishing details. All too often the final touches to a beautifully knitted garment are rushed in the euphoria of completing the project. By taking time with the detail of putting the pieces together a professional finish will be achieved. Weave in all the ends along the row at the back of the knitting, never up the side, as this will give bulky seams. Lay the pieces out flat on the wrong or reverse side and press the knitting with a steam iron or press gently under a damp cloth. Do not flatten the knitting or stretch it out of shape. When you have to join up sections of knitting, make sure you join each piece in turn, matching rows, and taking time to line up pieces accurately. Sewing stitches used in joining up should be neat and unobtrusive. (For further information on techniques, see page 125). Any trims or embellishments should be chosen with care to match both the colour and style of the garment and need to be securely attached to it.

giftwrapping ideas

Many of us are induced to knit for a baby when a close friend or relative becomes pregnant. If you want to offer something you have knitted to a friend or relative as a gift to welcome the newborn baby, do take care to present it beautifully. It becomes a token of your love and esteem, and will be very much appreciated. Nothing is too good for the new baby!

The best way to wrap any kind of present is with simplicity and style. Make sure that the knitted garment or project is neatly folded, ideally layered with tissue paper to prevent it creasing. Choose plain good-quality papers for wrapping, and find novel forms of tie, rather than the ubiquitous cheap ribbon. If you wrap the gift carefully, you can avoid the use of sticky tape, and the paper is then reusable. String, raffia or unusual ribbons can be used instead to package the parcel. Why not add a small additional present, in the shape of a baby's rattle or a small charm, as a finishing detail, tied to the ribbon? And don't forget to add a matching tag with a special message of congratulations. You can make these yourself very easily from pieces of card.

helpful information

care of yarns

A BABY'S SKIN IS SOFT, delicate and very sensitive, and great care should be taken in the laundering of their clothes. One thing is certain; baby clothes will require frequent washing. The yarn you use must be able to stand up to this frequent washing, but this does not necessarily mean that all yarns must be machine washable.

Look at the labels: those on most commercial yarns have instructions for washing or dry cleaning, drying and pressing. So for a project knitted in one yarn only, a quick look at the yarn label will tell you how to care for it. If you wish to work with several yarns in one piece of work, the aftercare requires a little more thought. If one label suggests dry cleaning, then be sure to dry clean the garment.

If in doubt about whether your knitting is washable, then make a little swatch of the yarns. Wash this to see if the fabric is affected by being immersed in water or not, watching out for shrinkage and stretching. If you are satisfied with the results, go ahead and wash the knitting by hand in lukewarm water. Never use hot water, as this will "felt" your fabric, and you will not be able to return it to its pre-washed state. Take care, too, to keep the rinsing water the same temperature as the washing water. Wool, in particular, tends to react to major changes in temperature.

Natural fibres such as wool, cotton and silk are usually better washed by hand, and in pure soap, than in a machine. Soap flakes are kinder to baby's skin than that of most detergents, provided all traces of the soap are removed in the rinsing process.

Washing: When washing the finished knitting, handle it carefully. There should be enough water to cover the garment completely and the soap should be thoroughly dissolved before immersing it. If you need to sterilize any garment that has become badly soiled or stained, then use a proprietary brand of sterilizer for this purpose.

Rinsing: Squeeze out excess water, never wring it out. Rinse thoroughly, until every trace of soap is removed, as any left in will matt the fibres and may irritate the baby's skin. Use at least two changes of water or continue until the water is clear and without bubbles.

Spinning: The garments can be rinsed on a short rinse and spin as part of a normal washing machine programme for delicate fabrics.

As a precaution, test wash any ribbons or trims you use before you make up the garment with them. Nothing is more infuriating than to spoil an entire garment because the trim colours run in the wash!

Drying: Squeeze the garment between towels or fold in a towel and gently spin.

Do not hang wet knitting up, as the weight of the water will stretch it out of shape. To dry, lay the knitting out flat on top of a towel, or an old terry nappy (diaper) which will absorb some of the moisture. Ease the garment into shape. Dry away from direct heat and leave flat until completely dry.

Pressing: When the garment is dry, ease it into shape. Check the yarn label before pressing your knitting as most fibres only require a little steam, and the iron should be applied gently. Alternatively, press with a damp cloth between the garment and the iron.

Removing stains: Stains are a fact of life in bringing up baby. Most of the stains that are likely to affect a baby's clothing are to do with foods. The best solution with any stain is to remove the garment while the stain is still wet and soak it thoroughly in cold, not hot, water. Failing that use a proprietary stain remover.

opposite: Natural fibres such as wool, cotton and silk are usually better washed by hand. Wash the finished knitting carefully and rinse thoroughly, before drying it flat on a rack.

sizing tables

INSTRUCTIONS are given in three sizes for each project; the figures for the larger sizes are given inside brackets. Sizes are given in ages and weight but are intended as an average guide only. More detailed measurements for body length, body width and sleeve length for each project are given in the following tables.

above: The pattern for the classic cashmere sweater can be found on page 20 and the pattern for the matching leggings on page 26.

right: The pattern for the classic cashmere bootees can be found on page 32.

classic cashmere sweater

TO FIT SIZES	1	2	3
BABY AGED (MONTHS)	0–3	3–6	6–9
FINISHED CHEST CM (IN)	48 (19)	55 (21½)	62 (24½)
BACK LENGTH CM (IN)	21.5 (8½)	25 (10)	29 (11½)

classic cashmere leggings

TO FIT SIZES	1	2	3
BABY AGED (MONTHS)	0–3	3–6	6–9
HIP CM (IN)	53 (21)	57 (22½)	60 (23½)
INSIDE LEG CM (IN)	24 (9½)	27 (10½)	29 (11½)

classic cashmere bootees

TO FIT SIZES	1	2	3
BABY AGED (MONTHS)	0–3	3–6	6–9
FOOT LENGTH CM (IN)	9 (3½)	10.5 (4⅛)	12 (4¾)

right: The pattern for the garter stitch cardigan can be found on page36.

centre: The pattern for the chunky knit cardigan can be found on page 50.

below: The pattern for the baby's beanie hat can be found on page 54

garter stitch cardigan

TO FIT SIZES	1	2	3
BABY AGED (MONTHS)	0-3	3-6	6-9
FINISHED CHEST CM (IN)	46 (18)	52 (20½)	58 (23)
BACK LENGTH CM (IN)	21(8¼)	23 (9)	25 (9¾)
SLEEVE LENGTH FROM CENTRE BACK CM (IN)	20 (8)	23 (9)	25 (10)

chunky knit cardigan

TO FIT SIZES	1	2	3
BABY AGED (MONTHS)	0-3	3-6	6-9
FINISHED CHEST CM (IN)	46 (18)	52 (20½)	58 (23)
BACK LENGTH CM (IN)	19 (7½)	21 (8½)	23 (9)
SLEEVE LENGTH FROM CENTRE BACK CM (IN)	28 (11)	30 (11¾)	32 (12½)

baby's beanie hat

TO FIT SIZES	1	2	3
BABY AGED (MONTHS)	0-3	3-6	6-9
HEAD CIRCUMFERENCE CM (IN)	34 (13½)	38 (15)	42 (16½)

right: The pattern for the garter stitch wrap top can be found on page 58

centre: The pattern for the vintage cardigan can be found on page 66.

below: The pattern for the garter stitch silk slippers can be found on page 80.

garter stitch wrap top

TO FIT SIZES	1	2	3
BABY AGED (MONTHS)	0-3	3-6	6-9
FINISHED CHEST CM (IN)	35.5(14)	40.5(16)	46(18)
BACK LENGTH CM (IN)	16.5 (6½)	19(7½)	21.5(8½)

vintage cardigan

TO FIT SIZES	1	2	3
BABY AGED (MONTHS)	0-3	3-6	6-9
FINISHED CHEST CM (IN)	48 (19)	53(21)	58(23)
BACK LENGTH CM (IN)	20 (8)	23(9)	25.5(10)
SLEEVE SEAM CM (IN)	14 (5½)	17 (6½)	19 (7½)

garter stitch silk slippers

TO FIT SIZES	1	2	3
BABY AGED (MONTHS)	0-3	3-6	6-9
FINISHED FOOT LENGTH CM (IN)	9 (3½)	10 (4)	11 (4¼)

right: The pattern for the traditional mabel dress can be found on page 84.

centre: The pattern for the ribbon-tied wool vest can be found on page 90.

below: The pattern for the rosebud cardigan can be found on page 96.

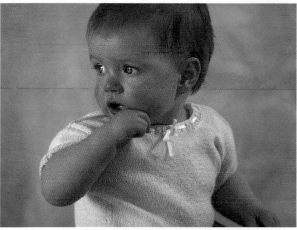

traditional mabel dress

TO FIT SIZES	1	2	3
BABY AGED (MONTHS)	0–3	3–6	6–9
LENGTH CM (IN)	30 (12)	33 (13)	11 (14¼)
FINSIHED CHEST (AROUND YOKE)	43 (17)	46 (18)	48.5 (19)

ribbon-tied wool vest

TO FIT SIZES	1	2	3
BABY AGED (MONTHS)	0–3	3–6	6–9
FINISHED CHEST CM (IN)	37 (14½)	42 (16½)	47 (18½)
LENGTH FROM SHOULDER CM (IN)	21.5 (8½)	24 (9½)	26.5 (10½)

rosebud cardigan

TO FIT SIZES	1	2	3
BABY AGED (MONTHS)	0–3	3–6	6–9
ACTUAL CHEST CM (IN)	46 (18)	51 (20)	56 (22)
BACK LENGTH CM (IN)	18 (7)	22 (8½)	26 (10)
SLEEVE LENGTH FROM CENTRE BACK CM (IN)	10 (4)	13 (5)	15 (6)

charts

SOME PATTERNS IN THIS BOOK require charts. Each square on the charts shown here represents a stitch and each horizontal line of squares on each chart represents a row of knitting.

When reading from the charts read odd-numbered rows as knit rows (from right to left) and read even-numbered rows as purl rows (from left to right).

For ease in reading charts it may be helpful to have the chart enlarged at a printers and then make any markings, such as row numbers, or notes that you may require as you work.

An alphabet is depicted here for working the baby blanket and baby cushion but you can use it for working alternative names or messages to personalize your projects. Each letter block is 24 stitches wide and 30 rows high, and is knitted in reverse stocking (stockinette) stitch, ie purl on the knit rows and knit on the purl rows. To work the letters start reading at the bottom right hand corner marked by ⌐ see B, D and F, or the edge of the letter, see A, C and E.

Similarly charts are given for the Cashmere teddy bear (page 123), should you find it easier to work from a chart than follow the written instructions. The Sssh baby sleeping chart (page 123) is for counted cross stitch embroidery, the centre being on the bottom row of bébé between é and b above the X.

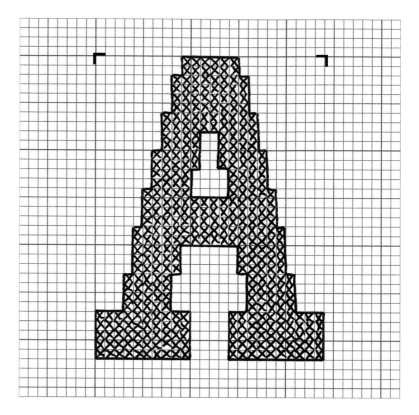

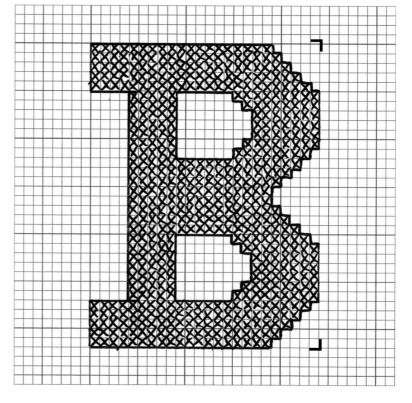

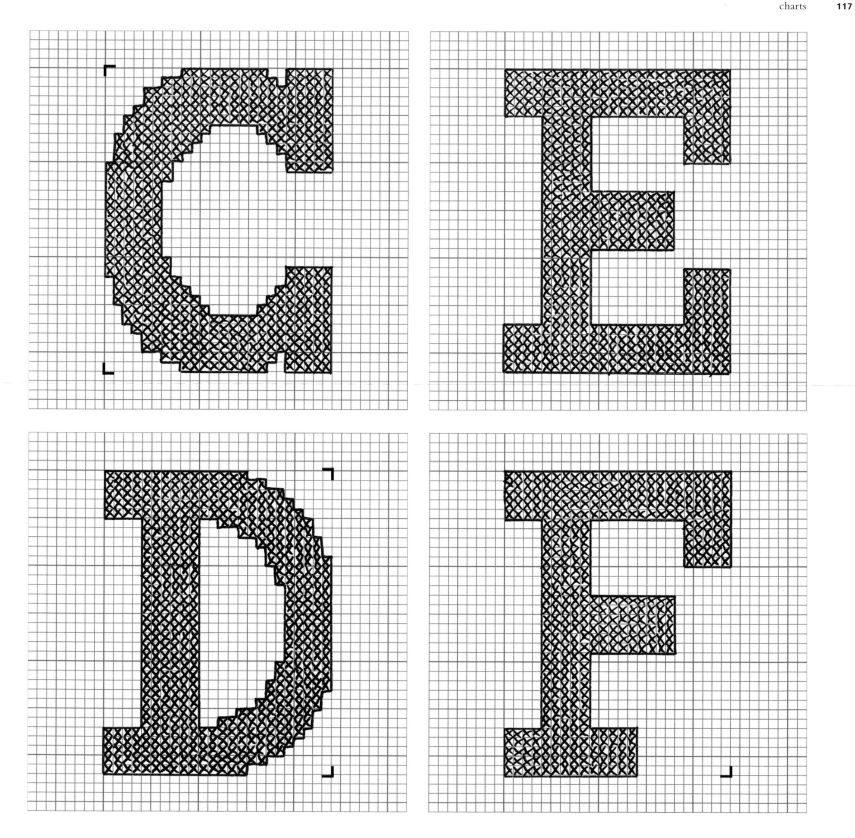

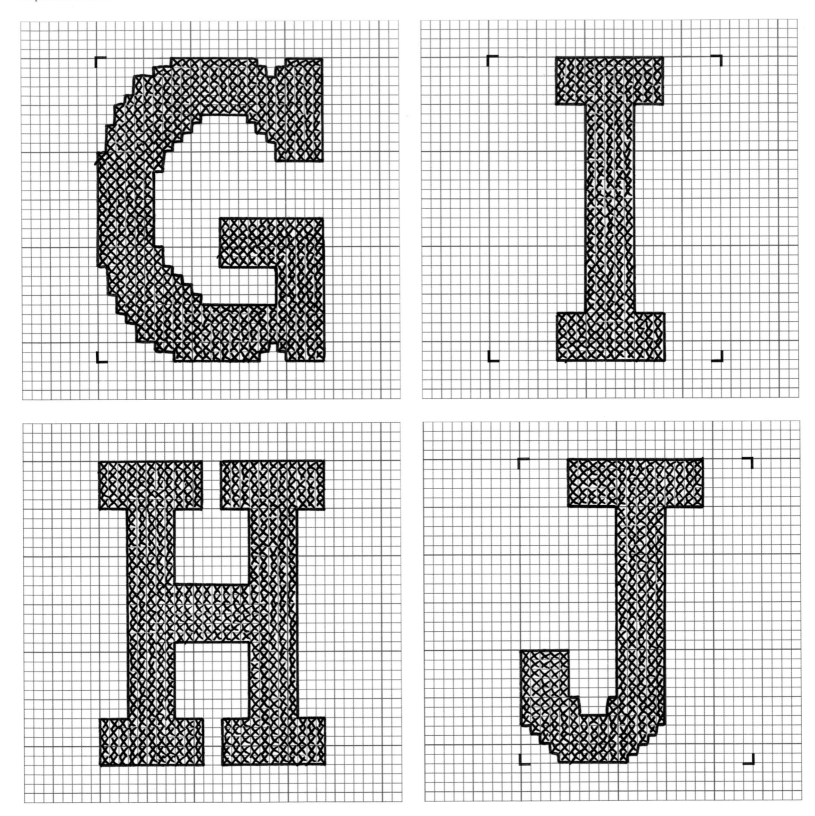

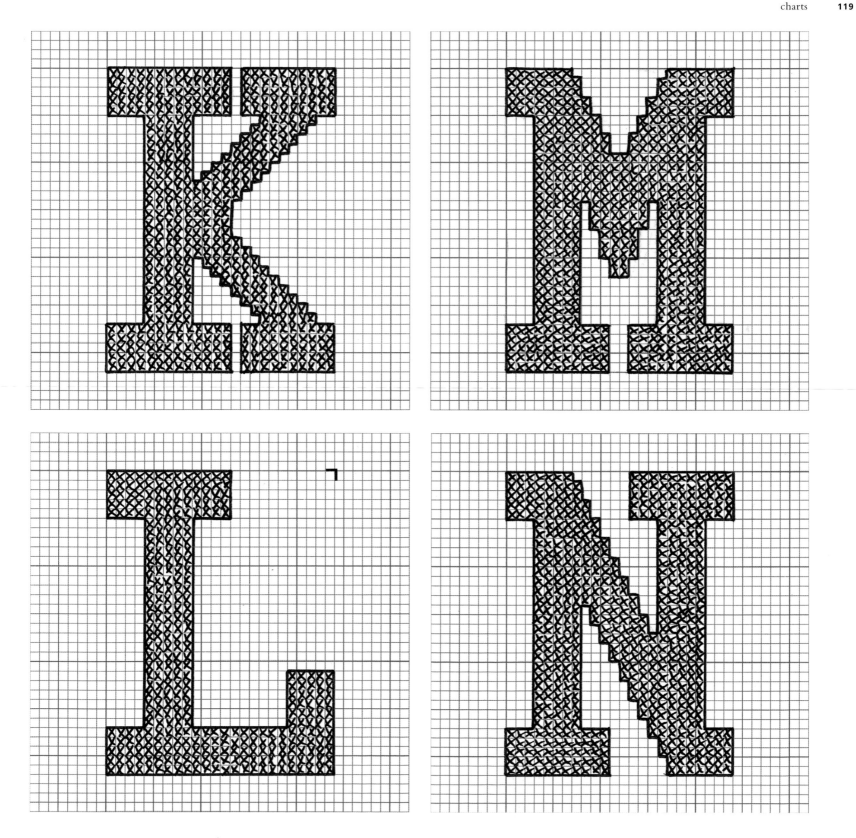

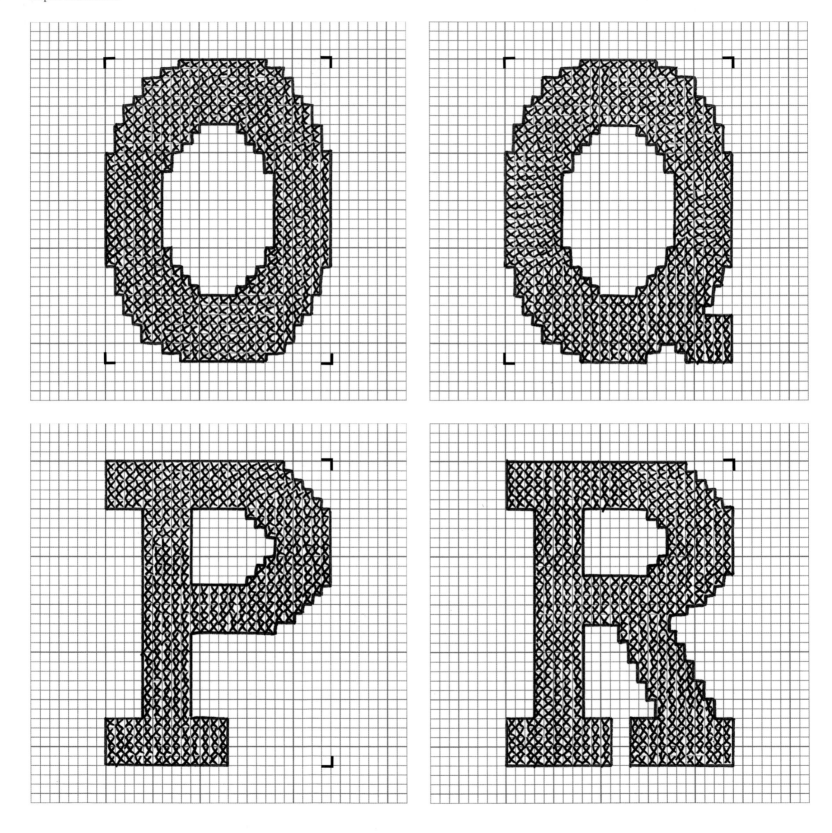

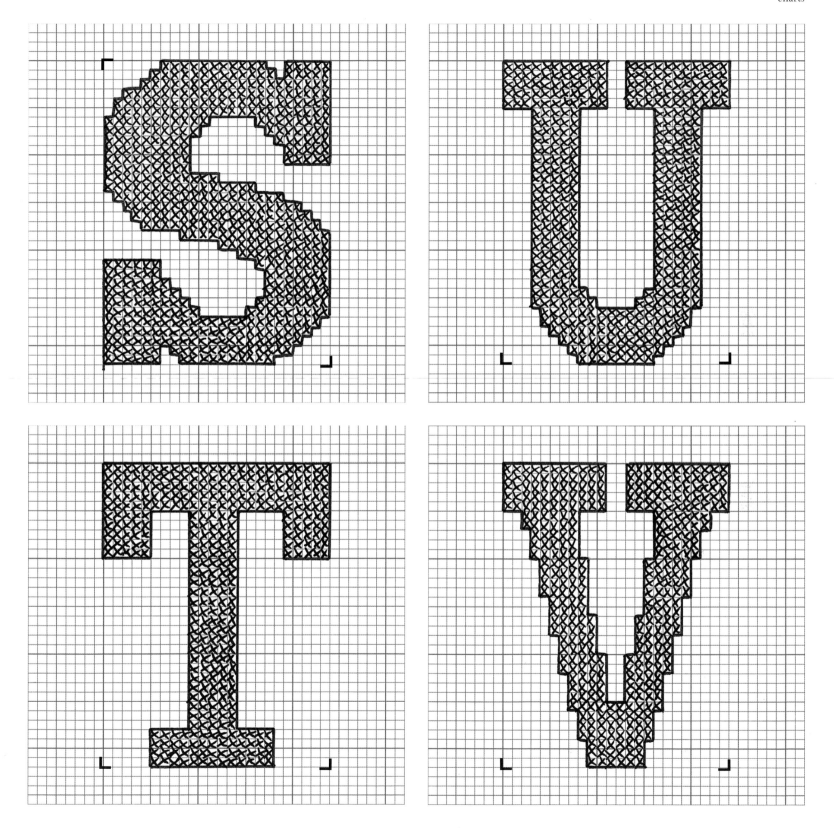

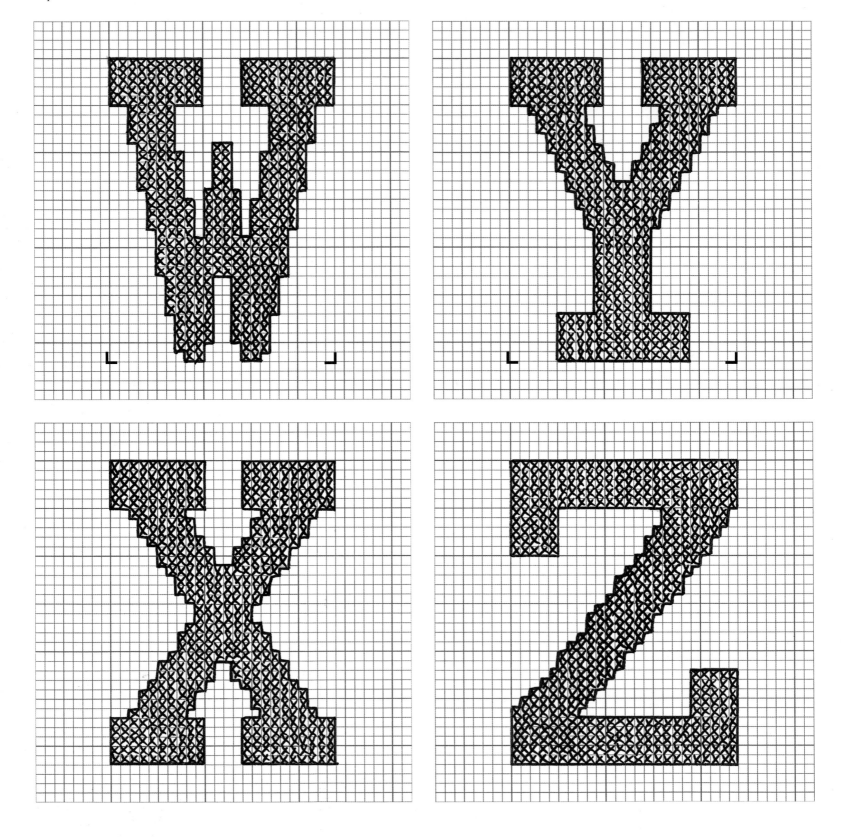

D

D

(c)

cashmere teddy bear

HEAD

C

41 rows

36 stitches

sssh! baby sleeping cushion

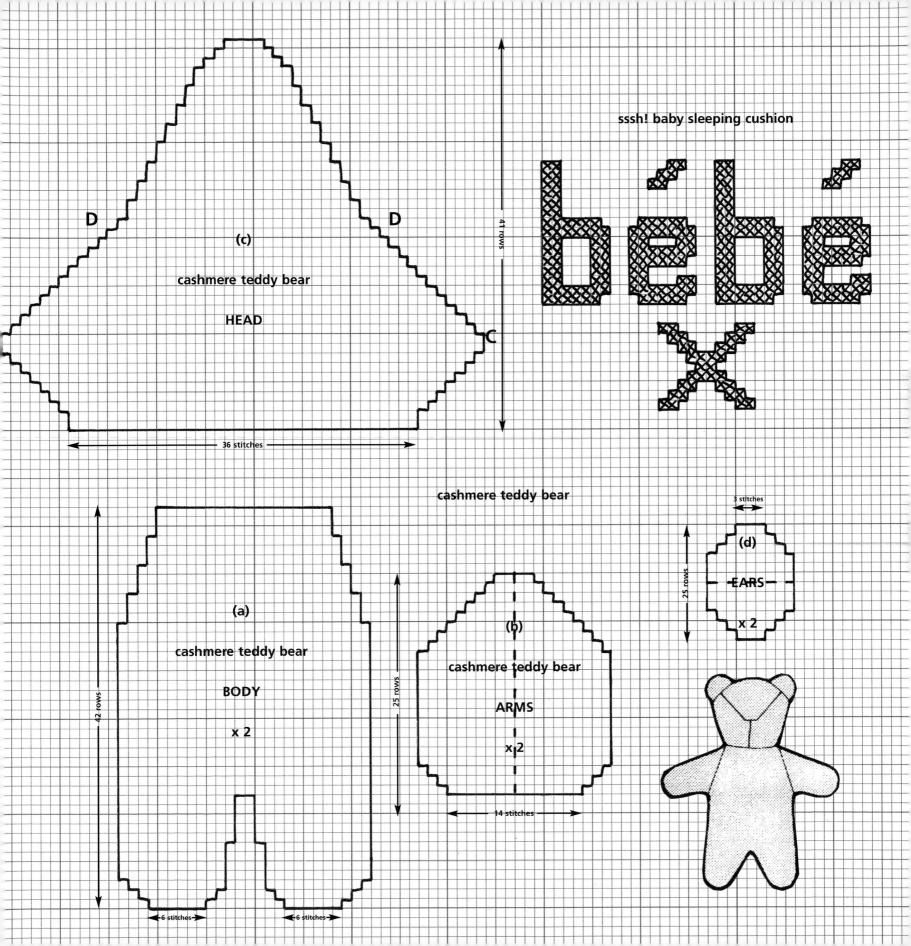

bébé

x

cashmere teddy bear

3 stitches

(d)

EARS

x 2

25 rows

(a)

cashmere teddy bear

BODY

x 2

42 rows

6 stitches   6 stitches

(b)

cashmere teddy bear

ARMS

x 2

25 rows

14 stitches

yarn buying information

THE SECRET TO GETTING the most out of a yarn is to experiment with it, trying out various needles sizes and seeing how it works in different stitch patterns.

I have recommended or suggested a yarn type for each project, which is of good quality and specifically suited to baby garments.

If you cannot find the particular yarn specified or suggested in the instructions, any other make of yarn that is of the same weight and type should serve as well, but, to avoid disappointing results, it is very important that you work a tension swatch first that matches that given in each project, changing the needle size if necessary to achieve the correct tension.

Substituting yarns: If you decide to use an alternative yarn, in order to find a specific shade or because you cannot obtain the yarn recommended, be sure to purchase a substitute yarn that is as close as possible to the original in thickness, weight and texture so that it will be compatible with the knitting instructions.

Buy one ball only to start with, so you can test the effect and the tension. Calculate quantities required using information about lengths, yardage or meterage found on the ball bands.

Actual yarns used: The following is a list of the yarns used for the projects in the book. The yarn characteristics given will be helpful if you are trying to find an alternative yarn.

FINE YARNS:

Jaeger silk 4 ply: a 4 ply silk yarn (100% pure silk), approximately 186m (201yds) per 50g ball.

Recommended tension is 28 stitches and 38 rows to 10 cm (4in) using 3mm (US 2-3) needles.

Jaeger matchmaker merino 4ply: a 4 ply wool yarn (100% merino wool), approximately 183m (200 yds) per 50g ball.

Recommended tension is 28 stitches and 36 rows to 10 cm (4in) using 3^1/$_4$mm (US 3) needles.

Rowan true 4 ply botany: a 4 ply wool yarn (100% pure new wool), approximately 170m (185 yd) per 50g ball.

Recommended tension is 28 stitches and 36 rows to 10 cms (4in) using 3^1/$_4$mm (US 3) needles.

Jaeger Siena 4ply: a 4 ply mercerized cotton yarn (100% pure cotton), approximately 140m (153yds) per 50g ball.

Recommended tension is 28 stitches and 38 rows to 10 cm (4in) using 2^3/$_4$-3mm [US 2-3] needles.

MEDIUM YARNS:

Jaeger cashmere: a 4 ply yarn, but knits as a double knitting weight yarn (90% cashmere, 10% polyamide), approximately 98m (107 yd) per 50g ball.

Recommended tension is 28 stitches and 36 rows to 10 cm (4in) using 3^1/$_4$mm (US 3) needles.

Rowan wool/cotton: a double knitting weight blend yarn (50% merino wool, 50% cotton), approximately 113m (123 yd) per 50g ball.

Recommended tension is 22-24 stitches and 30-32 rows to 10 cm (4in) using 3^3/$_4$-4 mm (US 5-6) needles.

Jaeger aqua cotton DK: a double knitting weight cotton yarn (100% mercerized cotton), approximately 106m (115yd) per 50g ball.

Recommended tension is 22 stitches and 30 rows to 10 cm (4in) using 4 mm (US 6) needles.

CHUNKY YARNS:

Rowan all seasons cotton: An Arran or chunky weight yarn (60% cotton, 40% acrylic), approximately 90m (98yds) per 50g ball.

Recommended tension is 16-18 stitches and 23-25 rows to 10 cm (4in) using 4^1/$_2$-5^1/$_2$mm (US 7-9) needles.

technique glossary

A FEW SPECIAL TECHNIQUES are used throughout the patterns in this book. For those who are unfamiliar with them, a brief explanation follows.

KNITTING TECHNIQUES:

Slip the first stitch

Transfer the stitch from the left needle to the right needle without knitting it.

Through the back loops

Put the right needle through the back loops of the next 2 stitches and knit or purl them together as though they were 1 stitch. On a purl row this takes a little practice.

Increase

Knit or purl the next stitch but do not drop it off the needle. Slip the point of the right needle through the back of the stitch and knit another stitch in the usual way, then drop the stitch from the left needle. You have made 2 stitches out of 1 stitch.

Decrease

Knit or purl the next 2 stitches together. You have made 1 stitch out of 2 stitches.

Yarn forward

Used to make a 'hole'. Bring yarn forward as if to purl, take it back over the right needle, then work the next instruction.

Yarn over

Used to make a 'hole'. Take yarn over right needle, from front to back of work and then under the right needle to the front of work, then work the next instruction.

Pick up stitches

Insert the right needle through the stitch or short loop along the edge of the piece of knitting to be attached and knit a stitch in the usual way. Do this, evenly spaced, for the required number of stitches.

Up 1 stitch

Make a stitch without leaving a hole by putting the right needle under the horizontal thread before the next stitch and placing this thread onto the left needle to make a stitch. Knit it through the back loop.

Chart reading

Each small square represents a stitch and a row. In knitting, read the knit rows from right to left and the purl rows from left to right.

SEWING TECHNIQUES:

Invisible seaming

Work with right sides facing, a blunt needle and the same yarn as the work. Place both pieces to be joined side by side, edges butted up, and, beginning at the lower edge, insert the needle down through the centre of a knitted stitch and then back up through centre of the stitch next to it. Repeat this action in the edge of the adjoining piece. Returning to the first piece, insert the needle down through the stitch it came out of, then back up through centre of next stitch to it. Repeat this zigzag action for the length of the entire seam, gently pulling the seam into shape as you work.

Mattress stitch

This is another name for invisible seaming (see instructions above).

suppliers

KNITTING YARNS: Full descriptions of the yarns used for the projects are given on page 124. Many of the projects in the book were worked in Rowan yarns; details for contacting Rowan Yarns and a list of selected stockists in the United Kingdom are provided below.

UNUSUAL 'YARNS' & ACCESSORIES: Other materials used for the projects are widely available in, craft shops or haberdasheries.

ROWAN YARNS WEBSITE
Contact the Rowan Yarns website for a complete list of stockists in the United Kingdom and for stockists in other countries.
www.rowanyarns.co.uk

ROWAN YARNS HEADQUARTERS
Rowan Yarns, Green Lane Mill, Holmfirth, West Yorkshire HD7 1RW, England.
Tel: 01484 681 881

SELECTED ROWAN STOCKISTS
Stockists in **bold type** are Rowan dedicated shops or departments, many offering professional help and mail-order facilities.

BATH AND NORTHEAST SOMERSET
BATH: **ROWAN AT Stitch Shop,** 15 The Podium, Northgate. Tel: 01225 481134
BRISTOL
BRISTOL: **ROWAN AT John Lewis,** Cribbs Causeway. Tel: 0117 959 1100
BEDFORDSHIRE
LEIGHTON BUZZARD: **ROWAN AT Needle & Thread,** 2/3 Peacock Mews. Tel: 01525 376456
BERKSHIRE
NEWBURY: Camp Hopson & Co Ltd, 6–12 Northbrook Street. Tel: 01635 523523
READING: **ROWAN AT Heelas,** Broad St. Tel: 01189 575955
SOUTH ASCOT: South Ascot Wools, 18 Brockenhurst Rd. Tel: 01344 628327
WINDSOR: Caleys, 19 High St.
Tel: 01753 863241

BUCKINGHAMSHIRE
MILTON KEYNES: **ROWAN AT John Lewis,** Central Milton Keynes. Tel: 01908 679171
CAMBRIDGESHIRE
CAMBRIDGE: **ROWAN AT Robert Sayle,** St Andrews St. Tel: 01223 361292
PETERBOROUGH: John Lewis, Queensgate Centre. Tel: 01733 344644
CHESHIRE
CHEADLE: John Lewis, Wilmslow Rd.
Tel: 0161 491 4914
HALE, ALTRINCHAM: Yvonne's Knitting Club. Tel: 0161 941 2534.
Mail order. 24hr ansphone.
Email: sales@internetwoolshop.com
CORNWALL
PENZANCE: Iriss, 66 Chapel St.
Tel: 01736 366568
ST. IVES: Antiques, Buttons & Crafts, 3A Tregenna Hill. Tel: 01736 793713
WADEBRIDGE: **ROWAN AT Artycrafts,** 41 Molesworth St. Tel: 01208 812274
CUMBRIA
CARLISLE: Pingouin, 20 Globe La.
Tel: 01228 520681
COCKERMOUTH: Silkstone, 12 Market Place. Tel: 01900 821 052.
Fax: 01900 821 051. Mail order
PENRITH: **ROWAN AT Indigo,** 7 Devonshire Arcade. Tel: 01768 899917
DEVON
PLYMOUTH: **ROWAN AT Dingles,** 40–46 Royal Parade. Tel: 01752 266611
TAVISTOCK: Knitting Image, 9 Pepper St. Tel: 01822 617410
TOTNES: Sally Carr Designs, The Yarn Shop, 31 High St. Tel: 01803 863060
DORSET
BRIDPORT: Harlequin, 76 West St.
Tel: 01308 456449
CHRISTCHURCH: Honora, 69 High St.
Tel: 01202 486000
DORCHESTER: Goulds Ltd., 22 South St. Tel: 01305 217816
SHERBORNE: Hunters of Sherborne, 4 Tilton Court, Digby Rd. Tel: 01935 817722
STURMINSTER NEWTON: Hansons Fabrics, Station Rd. Tel: 01258 472698
WIMBORNE: **ROWAN AT The Walnut**

Tree, 1 West Borough. Tel: 01202 840722
DURHAM
DARLINGTON: **ROWAN AT Binns,** 7 High Row. Tel: 01325 462606
ESSEX
CHELMSFORD: Franklins, 219 Moulsham St. Tel: 01245 346300
COLCHESTER: Franklins, 13/15 St Botolphs St. Tel: 01206 563955
MALDON: Peachey Ethknits, 6/7 Edwards Walk. Tel: 01621 857102 Mail order. Email: peachey-ethknits@ndirect.co.uk
SOUTHEND-ON-SEA: Gades, 239 Churchill South, Victoria Circus. Tel: 01702 613789
GLOUCESTERSHIRE
CHELTENHAM: **ROWAN AT Cavendish House,** The Promenade. Tel: 01242 521300
CIRENCESTER: Ashley's Wool Specialist, 62 Dyer St. Tel: 01285 653245. Mail order
GREATER MANCHESTER
DIDSBURY: Sew In, 741 Wilmslow Rd.
Tel: 0161 445 5861
MARPLE: Sew In, 46 Market St.
Tel: 0161 427 2529
HAMPSHIRE
ALRESFORD: Designer Knits, The Gable House, New Farm Rd.
Tel: 01962 733499
BASINGSTOKE: Pack Lane Wool Shop, 171 Pack Lane, Kempshott. Tel: 01256 323644
LYMINGTON: Leigh's, 56 High St.
Tel: 01590 673254
SOUTHAMPTON: Tyrrell & Green, Tel: 01703 227711
SOUTHSEA: Knight & Lee, Palmerston Rd. Tel: 01705 827511
TWYFORD: Riverside Yarns, Cockscombe Farm, Watley Lane. Tel: 01962 714380
WINCHESTER: C & H Fabrics, 8 High St. Tel: 01962 843355
HEREFORDSHIRE
HEREFORD: Singer Needlecrafts, 14 Maylord St. Tel: 01432 358986
HERTFORDSHIRE
BOREHAM WOOD: The Wool Shop, 92 Shenley Rd. Tel: 0181 905 2499.
Mail order
WATFORD: **ROWAN AT Trewins,** The Harlequin, High St. Tel: 01923 244266
WELWYN GARDEN CITY: **ROWAN AT**

John Lewis. Tel: 01707 323456
KENT
ASHFORD: Katie's Workbox, 15 High St, Headcorn. Tel: 01622 891065
CANTERBURY: ROWAN AT C & H Fabrics, 2 St. George's St. Tel: 01227 459760
GREENHITHE: John Lewis Bluewater. Tel: 01322 624123
MAIDSTONE: C & H Fabrics, 68 Week St. Tel: 01622 762060
ROCHESTER: **ROWAN AT Francis Iles,** 73 High St. Tel: 01634 843082
TUNBRIDGE WELLS: C & H Fabrics, 113/115 Mount Pleasant. Tel: 01892 522618
LANCASHIRE
ACCRINGTON: Sheila's Wool Shop, 284 Union Rd, Oswaldtwistle.
Tel: 01254 875525. Email: sheilaswoolshop@compuserve.com
ST ANNE'S-ON-SEA: **ROWAN AT Kathleen Barnes,** 22 The Crescent.
Tel/fax: 01253 724194
LEICESTERSHIRE
OAKHAM: **ROWAN AT The Wool Centre,** 40 Melton Rd. Tel: 01572 757574.
Knitting up service available
LINCOLNSHIRE
LOUTH: Tudor Wool Shop, 13 Queen St. Tel: 01507 604037
LONDON - CENTRAL
EC1: Debbie Bliss, 365 St John St, EC1V 4LB Tel: 020 7833 8255
SW1: **ROWAN AT Peter Jones,** Sloane Square, SW1. Tel: 020 7730 3434
W1: **ROWAN AT Liberty,** Regent St, W1. Tel: 020 7734 1234
W1: **ROWAN AT John Lewis,** Oxford St, W1. Tel: 020 7629 7711
W2: **ROWAN AT Colourway,** 112A Westbourne Grove, W2.
Tel/fax: 020 7229 1432. 24hr ansphone.
Email: shop@colourway.co.uk
W4: Creations, 29 Turnham Green Terrace, Chiswick, W4 1RS. Tel: 020 7747 9697.
Mail order
LONDON - NORTH & WEST
NW4: **ROWAN AT John Lewis,** Brent Cross Shopping Centre, NW4.
Tel: 020 8202 6535
W13: Bunty's at Daniels, 96/122 Uxbridge Rd,

West Ealing, W13 9RA. Tel: 020 8567 8729

LONDON - SOUTH

BARNES: Creations, 79 Church Rd, SW13.
Tel: 020 8563 2970. Mail Order

PENGE: Maple Textiles, 188/190 Maple Rd.
Tel: 020 8778 8049

MERSEYSIDE

LIVERPOOL: **ROWAN AT George Henry Lee,** Basnett St. Tel: 0151 709 7070

NORFOLK

ROUGHTON: **ROWAN AT Sew Creative,**
Groveland Farm, Thorpe Market Rd.
Tel: 01263 834021

NORWICH: Bonds, All Saints Green.
Tel: 01603 660021

NORTHUMBERLAND

CORBRIDGE: The Fabric & Tapestry Shop,
Sydgate House, Middle St.
Tel: 01434 632902. Mail order

NOTTINGHAMSHIRE

NEWARK: Chameleon, 33–35 Cartergate.
Tel: 01636 671803. Ansaphone

NOTTINGHAM: **ROWAN AT Jessops,**
Victoria Centre. Tel: 0115 9418282

OXFORDSHIRE

BURFORD: Burford Needlecraft Shop, 117
High St. Tel: 01993 822136. Mail order

OXFORD: **ROWAN AT Rowan,** 102
Gloucester Green. Tel: 01865 793366.
24hr ansphone

SHROPSHIRE

SHREWSBURY: **ROWAN AT House of Needlework,** 11 Wyle Cop.
Tel: 01743 355533 (formerly Osa)

SOMERSET

BURNHAM-ON-SEA: The Woolsack, 7
College St. Tel: 01278 784443

GLASTONBURY: Penny Juniors, 40 High St.
Tel: 01458 831974

TAUNTON: Hayes Wools, 150 East Reach.
Tel: 01823 284768. Mail order

YEOVIL: Enid's Wool & Craft Shop, Church
St. Tel: 01935 412421

SUFFOLK

BURY ST EDMUNDS: **ROWAN AT Jaycraft,** 78 St John's St. Tel: 01284 752982

IPSWICH: Spare Moments, 13 Northgate St.
Tel: 01473 259876

SURREY

BANSTEAD: Maxime Wool & Craft Shop,

155 High St. Tel: 01737 352798

KINGSTON: **ROWAN AT John Lewis,**
Wood St. Tel: 0181 547 3000

GUILDFORD: **ROWAN AT Army & Navy,**
High St. Tel: 01483 568171

EAST SUSSEX

BATTLE: Battle Wool Shop, 2 Mount St. Tel:
01424 775073

BRIGHTON: C & H Fabrics, 179 Western
Rd. Tel: 01273 321959

EASTBOURNE: C & H Fabrics, 82/86
Terminus Rd. Tel: 01323 410503

EAST HOATHLEY (NR UCKFIELD): The Wool
Loft, Upstairs at Clara's, 9 High St.
Tel: 01825 840339. Mail order.
Email: Claras@netway.co.uk

LEWES: **ROWAN AT Kangaroo,** 70 High
St. Tel: 01273 478554

WEST SUSSEX

ARUNDLE: **ROWAN AT David's Needle-Art,** 37 Tarrant St. Tel: 01903 882761

BURGESS HILL: The Fabric Shop, 29 The
Martlets. Tel: 01444 236688. Mail order

CHICHESTER: C & H Fabrics, 33/34 North
St. Tel: 01243 783300

HORSHAM: The Fabric Shop, 62 Swan Walk.
Tel: 01403 217945

SHOREHAM BY SEA: **ROWAN AT
Shoreham Knitting,** 19 East St.
Tel: 01273 461029. Fax: 01273 465407.
Email: skn@sure-employ.demon.co.uk

WORTHING: **ROWAN AT The Fabric
Shop,** 55 Chapel Rd. Tel: 01903 207389

TEESIDE

HARTLEPOOL: Bobby Davison, 101 Park Rd.
Tel: 01429 861300.
Email: mail@woolsworldwide.com

TYNE & WEAR

GATESHEAD: **ROWAN AT House of
Fraser,** Metro Centre. Tel: 0191 493 2424

NEWCASTLE UPON TYNE: **ROWAN AT
Bainbridge,** Eldon Square. Tel: 0191 232 5000

NEWCASTLE UPON TYNE: **ROWAN AT
Fenwick Limited,** 39 Northumberland St.
Tel: 0191 232 5100

WARWICKSHIRE

WARWICK: Warwick Wools, 17 Market Place.
Tel: 01926 492853

WEST MIDLANDS

BIRMINGHAM: **ROWAN AT Rackhams,**

Corporation St. Tel: 0121 236 3333

SOLIHULL: Stitches, 355 Warwick Road,
Olton. Tel: 0121 706 1048

WOLVERHAMPTON: **ROWAN AT Beatties,**
71–78 Victoria St. Tel: 01902 422311

WILTSHIRE

CALNE: Handi Wools, 3 Oxford Rd.
Tel: 01249 812081

SALISBURY: Stitches, Cross Keys Chequer.
Tel: 01722 411148. Mail order

WORCESTERSHIRE

KIDDERMINSTER: Woolwise, 10 Lower Mill
St. Tel: 01562 820279

NORTH YORKSHIRE

HELMSLEY: **ROWAN AT Tapestry
Garden,** 2 Castlegate. Tel: 01439 771300

SETTLE: Ancient & Modern, 39 Duke St.
Tel: 01729 824298

WHITBY: **ROWAN AT Bobbins,**
Wesley Hall, Church St.
Tel/fax: 01947 600585.
Email: bobbins@globalnet.co.uk

YORK: **ROWAN AT Craft Basics,**
9 Gillygate. Tel: 01904 652840

SOUTH YORKSHIRE

SHEFFIELD: ROWAN AT Cole Brothers,
Barkers Pool. Tel: 0114 2768511

WEST YORKSHIRE

HEBDEN BRIDGE: **ROWAN AT Attica,**
2 Commercial St. Tel: 01422 844327

HOLMFIRTH: **ROWAN AT Up Country,**
6 Market Walk. Tel/fax: 01484 687803.
Email: gpaul@upco.u-net.com

WALES

CARDIFF: **ROWAN AT David Morgan
Ltd,** 26 The Hayes. Tel: 01222 221011

CONWY: Ar-y-Gweill, 8 Heol Yr Orsaf,
Llanrwst. Tel: 01492 641149

FISHGUARD: Jane's of Fishguard, 14 High St.
Tel: 01348 874443

SWANSEA: Mrs Mac's, 2 Woodville Rd,
Mumbles. Tel: 01792 369820

SCOTLAND

ABERDEEN: John Lewis, George St.
Tel: 01224 625000

BEAULY: Linda Usher, 50 High St.
Tel: 01463 783017

CASTLE DOUGLAS: Needlecraft, 201 King St.
Tel: 01556 503606

CRIEF: Lint Mill Knitwear, 1 Dunira St,

Comrie. Tel: 01764 670300

EDINBURGH: **ROWAN AT John Lewis,**
St James Centre. Tel: 0131 556 9121

EDINBURGH: **ROWAN AT Jenners,**
48 Princes St. Tel: 0131 225 2442

EDINBURGH: **ROWAN AT Wooly
Mammoth,** 17 Jeffrey St, Off the Royal
Mile. Tel/fax: 0131 557 5025.
Email: mammoth@ednet.co.uk

GLASGOW: John Lewis, Buchanan Galleries.
Tel: 0141 353 6677

HUNTLY: **ROWAN AT Not Just Wool,**
9 Bogie St. Tel: 01466 799045

ISLE OF ARRAN: Trareoch Craft Shop,
Balmichael Visitors Centre, Shiskine.
Tel: 01770 860515

ISLE OF SKYE: Di Gilpin, The Old Mission
Hall, Struan Workshop, Struan.
Tel: 01470 572 284

LANARK: Strands, 8 Bloomgate. Tel: 01555
665757. Mail order

LINLITHGOW: Nifty Needles, 56 High St. Tel:
01506 670435

LONGNIDDRY: Longniddry Post Office, 29a
Links Rd. Tel: 01875 852894

SHETLAND ISLANDS: Wimberry, Gardens,
Skeld. Tel: 01595 860371. Mail order

KITS:

**Kits for certain projects are available
through Rowan's distributors. Please
contact your nearest stockist.
Alternatively email
erika@eka.demon.co.uk**

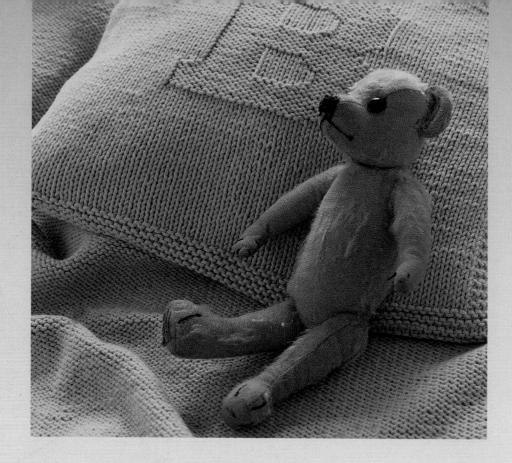

a c k n o w l e d g e m e n t s

This book is dedicated to the anonymous women who have knitted, stitched and created for their children, their children's children, and the children of their families and friends of successive generations. I have sought and bought their work from flea markets and charity shops the world over. Their love and care has been crafted into every fibre and stitch. Many of these women have had no formal training, just a passion for their craft, taught and passed down to them over the generations. They are my inspiration.

My sincerest thanks to the many people who have contributed to the creation of this book. They are a very special team, selected for their professionalism, enthusiasm, creativity, dedication, patience, attention to detail and endless support. I would like to thank, in particular, Susan Berry, John Heseltine, Debbie Mole, Eva Yates, Claire Waite Brown, Sally Lee, and Sarah Phillips. I would also like to thank Kate Kirby, Clare Lattin and Niamh Hatton at Collins & Brown, Shephen Sheard and the Rowan Yarns and Jaeger teams, Rosalynn Kennedy, Ian and Bella Harris and the mothers and babies who so kindly agreed to be photographed for this book, along with the teddy bear, kindly loaned by Debbie Mole. I would like to thank Claudia for the original inspiration.